CAMPAIGN • 241

THE FALL OF ENGLISH FRANCE 1449–53

DAVID NICOLLE

ILLUSTRATED BY GRAHAM TURNER

Series editor Marcus Cowper

First published in Great Britain in 2012 by Osprey Publishing,
Midland House, West Way, Botley, Oxford, OX2 0PH, UK
44-02 23rd Street, Suite 219, Long Island City, NY 11101, USA

Email: info@ospreypublishing.com

OSPREY PUBLISHING IS PART OF THE OSPREY GROUP.

A CIP catalogue record for this book is available from the British Library.

Print ISBN: 978 1 84908 616 5
PDF e-book ISBN: 978 1 84908 617 2
EPUB e-book ISBN: 978 1 78096 035 7

Editorial by Ilios Publishing Ltd, Oxford, UK (www.iliospublishing.com)
Design: The Black Spot
Index by Marie-Pierre Evans
Originated by Blenhiem Colour ltd
Cartography: Bounford.com
Bird's-eye view artworks: The Black Spot
Printed in China through Worldprint

12 13 14 15 16   10 9 8 7 6 5 4 3 2

DEDICATION

For Joy and Alex, contributing to the English 'reconquest' of the Dordogne?

ARTIST'S NOTE

Readers may care to note that the original paintings from which the
colour plates in this book were prepared are available for private sale.
The Publishers retain all reproduction copyright whatsoever.
All enquiries should be addressed to:

Graham Turner, PO Box 568, Aylesbury, Bucks, HP17 8EX, UK
www.studio88.co.uk

The Publishers regret that they can enter into no correspondence upon
this matter.

THE WOODLAND TRUST

Osprey Publishing are supporting the Woodland Trust, the UK's leading
woodland conservation charity, by funding the dedication of trees.

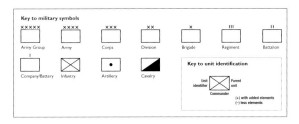

CONTENTS

ORIGINS OF THE CAMPAIGN   5

CHRONOLOGY   8

OPPOSING FORCES   10
The reformed French army of Charles VII . English armies in the mid-15th century
Morale and the rise of nationalism

OPPOSING COMMANDERS   17
French commanders . English commanders

THE FALL OF NORMANDY   22
The English invasion . From the Grand-Vey to Formigny . The battle of Formigny
The final collapse in Normandy

THE FALL OF GASCONY   42
The battle of Castillon . The end of English Gascony

AFTERMATH   84
The impact on France . The impact on England . Postscript in Calais

THE BATTLEFIELDS TODAY   92

FURTHER READING   93

INDEX   95

The decline of English France: frontiers *c.*1448

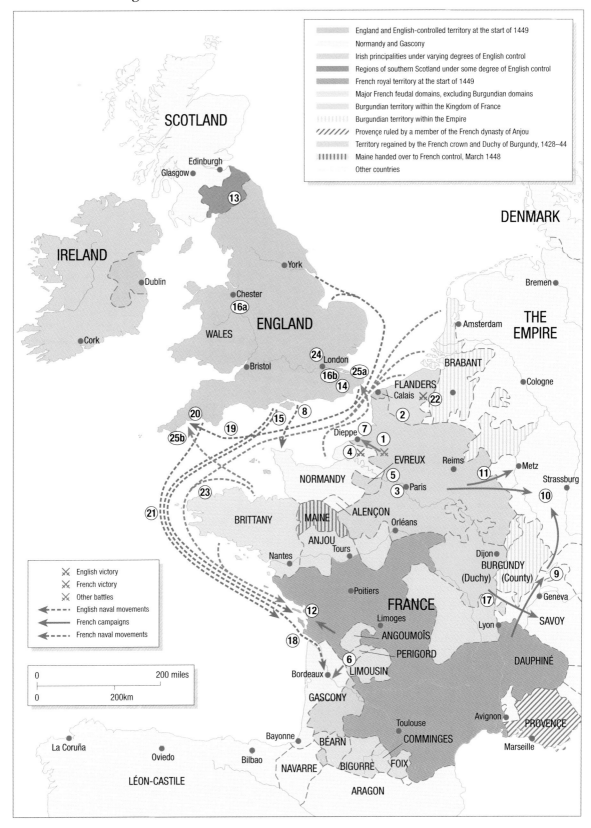

Legend:

- England and English-controlled territory at the start of 1449
- Normandy and Gascony
- Irish principalities under varying degrees of English control
- Regions of southern Scotland under some degree of English control
- French royal territory at the start of 1449
- Major French feudal domains, excluding Burgundian domains
- Burgundian territory within the Kingdom of France
- Burgundian territory within the Empire
- Provence ruled by a member of the French dynasty of Anjou
- Territory regained by the French crown and Duchy of Burgundy, 1428–44
- Maine handed over to French control, March 1448
- Other countries

- ✕ English victory
- ✕ French victory
- ✕ Other battles
- → English naval movements
- → French campaigns
- → French naval movements

0 ——— 200 miles
0 ——— 200km

SCOTLAND
Edinburgh
Glasgow
⑬

DENMARK

IRELAND
Dublin
Cork

York
Chester ⑯ₐ
ENGLAND
WALES
Bristol
⑳
㉕ᵦ
⑲
⑮
⑧
⑳
㉔ London
⑯ᵦ ㉕ₐ
⑭

Bremen
THE EMPIRE
Amsterdam
BRABANT
Cologne

FLANDERS
Calais ✕ ㉒
②
Dieppe ⑦
①
④ ✕
EVREUX
⑤
③ Paris
Reims
⑪ Metz
Strassburg
⑩

Bordeaux
NORMANDY
BRITTANY
㉓
MAINE
ALENÇON
ANJOU
Tours
Nantes

Orléans

Dijon
BURGUNDY
(Duchy) (County)
⑨
Geneva
⑰
SAVOY

Poitiers
FRANCE
Limoges
ANGOUMOÎS
PERIGORD
⑥
LIMOUSIN
⑫
⑱
Bordeaux
GASCONY
BÉARN
Bayonne
NAVARRE BIGORRE FOIX
ARAGON
Toulouse
COMMINGES
Avignon
PROVENCE
Marseille
DAUPHINÉ
Lyon

La Coruña
Oviedo
Bilbao
LÉON-CASTILE

ORIGINS OF THE CAMPAIGN

After a period of uneasy truce, the Hundred Years War flared up again early in the 15th century with yet another English invasion of France, marked by a crushing English victory at Agincourt in 1415, soon followed by the signing of an Anglo-Burgundian alliance. In 1418 the Burgundians took control of Paris and in 1420 the Treaty of Troyes recognized Henry V of England as heir to the aged and mentally unstable Charles VI of France. Henry V then married Catherine de Valois to unite the ruling houses of England and France. On the face of it England had won the war, but Charles VI's disinherited son, the Dauphin Charles, refused to recognize the treaty and established a rival court in the central French city of Bourges. This 'Kingdom of Bourges' was financially and militarily weak but became the centre of an increasingly effective resistance and, after Jeanne d'Arc had convinced the ex-dauphin, now the self-declared King Charles VII, into having himself crowned in the sacred city of Reims (see Campaign 94: *Orléans 1429*, Osprey Publishing Ltd: Oxford, 2001), the balance gradually shifted in his favour.

Charles VI of France and Henry V of England both died in 1422, leaving their theoretically joint Crown to the infant Henry, called the VI of England and the II of France (though this title is not accepted by French historians). The concept of two kingdoms coming together in such a personal union was widely accepted in late medieval Europe, and many English historians still

1 French defeat English at Gerberoy, spring 1435.
2 Alliance between Charles VII and the Duke of Burgundy confirmed at Arras, 1435.
3 English evacuate Paris, 1436.
4 English defeat French at Ry, 2 February 1436.
5 French retake Pontoise, 1441.
6 French threaten Gascony, 1441–42.
7 French retake Dieppe and an English attempt to retake it fails, 1443.
8 English army sails to Cherbourg from Portsmouth because French taking of Dieppe makes eastern part of English Channel unsafe.
9 The Dauphin Louis campaigns against the Swiss in support of Frederick of Hapsburg, 1444.
10 Charles VII and the Dauphin Louis campaign against *écorcheurs* in Alsace and Lorraine, 1444.
11 Charles VII leads punitive expedition against Metz in support of the Duke of Lorraine.
12 Major upgrading of fortifications at La Rochelle naval base, 1445–47.
13 English defeated by Scots in renewed hostilities, 1448–49.
14 Kentish rebellion led by Jack Cade reaches London but is crushed in July 1449.
15 English reinforcements under Richard Woodville Lord Rivers sent to Gascony, 1450.
16 Yorkist revolt in Ludlow (A) in February, stand-off between Yorkist and Royalist forces at Dartford is ended by negotiation (B) in March, 1452.
17 Charles VII marches against Savoy, August 1452.
18 English army under Talbot, initially mustered to support Calais, sails to retake Bordeaux from the French, September–October 1452.
19 Ships from Hull, King's Lynn and Dover assemble at Fowey for second expedition to Gascony, autumn and early winter 1452.
20 English fleet moves from Fowey to Plymouth, February 1453.
21 English army under John Viscount Lisle sails to support Talbot, March 1453.
22 Duke of Burgundy defeats Ghent rebels at the battle of Gavere, 23 July 1453.
23 Charles VII assembles ships from Holland, Zealand, Flanders, Brittany, Poitou and Spain at La Rochelle to support second French siege of Bordeaux, summer 1453.
24 First battle of Barnet, 22 May 1455 (start of Wars of the Roses).
25 French fleet attacks Sandwich (A) and Fowey (B), nominally in support of Lancastrians in the Wars of the Roses, 1457.

LEFT
A French illustration, made around 1460, showing the relationship between the kingdoms of England and France in French eyes, with King Richard I of England offering homage to King Philippe Auguste of France. (*Grand Chroniques de France*, Bib. Munic. Ms. 5, f.225v, Châteauroux)

RIGHT
Little remains of the French kings' fortified palace on the Isle de la Cité in Paris apart from three massive towers incorporated into the later Palais de Justice. (Author's photograph)

harbour a nostalgic feeling that it would have been a reasonable way to end the long conflict. Nevertheless, English and Burgundian armies failed to take control of the whole country, and the English faced huge difficulties maintaining order in the vast areas they ruled after the Treaty of Troyes. Whether this territory really formed an 'English France' during the 15th century remains controversial. Meanwhile, the English position in south-western France had hardly been affected by the great victories in the north. Here there was no significant expansion, and what might be called 'French France' under Charles VII still controlled the Mediterranean coast and an Atlantic coast between Gascony and Brittany. Then there was Brittany itself; this Duchy was a powerful military force that overlooked the strategic sea lanes between England and Gascony. Both sides were eager to draw Brittany into their fold, and Charles VII's eventual success in doing this was a major boost to his cause.

The apparently deep-seated pro-English sentiment in Gascony was in reality an attachment to local autonomy strengthened by commercial self-interest. Put simply, the people of Gascony preferred the distant rule of England to that of an increasingly centralizing and powerful French monarchy. The link between London and Bordeaux was particularly strong, English settlement in Gascony being primarily focused upon Bordeaux, Bayonne and Dax. Here the resident English included merchants and craftsmen as well as garrisons. Most seem to have been prosperous, with the only exceptions being some rural parishes where poorer English settlers may have been involved in wine growing.

Meanwhile the situation in England was surprisingly complex for a country that believed that it had won the war, with widespread criticism of the cult of royal militarism. Some even linked the war with the stories of King Arthur and prophesied that – as in the *Tales of the Knights of the Round Table* – all would end in catastrophe. The high hopes of King Edward III's reign had largely evaporated and an increasingly unpopular war had become a political burden for Henry VI's government. Even the King's marriage to another French princess, Margaret of Anjou, did little to raise the Crown's prestige, and the unfortunate Margaret was seen as an interfering foreigner.

The situation in France outside those regions under English rule was dominated by relations between the Duke of Burgundy and his cousin, King Charles VII. While the alliance between Burgundy and England endured, Charles VII had little hope of expelling the invaders and his struggle was as much diplomatic as military. There were also deep-seated tensions between other senior aristocratic families, not least between the houses of Bourbon and Burgundy. To further complicate the issue, the reforms that characterized Charles VII's reign were intended to strengthen the King's position, thus weakening that of the great nobles upon whom the King's military power ultimately rested.

Meanwhile the Duke of Brittany became a somewhat reluctant ally of Charles VII, largely owing to pressure from his brother, Arthur de Richemont, the Constable of France. Unlike their ruler, however, the people of Brittany remained strongly pro-French and furnished the royal armies with large numbers of committed troops. One major diplomatic triumph nevertheless trumped all others when, in 1435, the Duke of Burgundy changed sides and formed an alliance with Charles VII. This was seen as a betrayal in England, where Parliament approved a large sum of money to continue the war. On the other side, Burgundy's new stance meant that Charles VII's overstretched armies could focus on their struggle with the English in Normandy and Gascony.

The following year the English evacuated Paris, and in 1441 the French broke through to the English Channel, taking Pontoise, and then launching an offensive in the south-west. In 1443 the French took Dieppe, thus acquiring a major port in Upper Normandy and making English shipping in the Channel highly vulnerable. Indeed English armies sailing for France now tended to embark at Portsmouth rather than higher up the Channel, where the English were losing control of the sea.

Under such circumstances the truce agreed at Tours in 1444 came as a relief to the English, not least to those governing Normandy. It would be renewed until 1448, though in the meantime Henry VI secretly agreed to hand over the province of Maine – a move that would precipitate the final crisis.

CHRONOLOGY

1415 English defeat French at battle of Agincourt.

1416 Anglo-Burgundian alliance is signed at Calais following the assassination of Duke John the Fearless of Burgundy.

1418 Burgundians take control of Paris.

1420 Treaty of Troyes recognizes Henry V of England as heir to Charles VI of France; the Dauphin Charles is 'banished' (though only to Bourges); marriage of Henry V and Catherine de Valois.

1422 Deaths of Henry V and Charles VI; the one-year-old Henry VI is declared King of both England and France under separate regencies; the Dauphin declares himself King as Charles VII.

1429 French under the nominal command of Jeanne d'Arc raise the siege of Orléans, and defeat the English at Patay; Charles VII is crowned at Reims.

1431 Jeanne d'Arc is burned at Rouen; Henry VI is crowned King of France in Paris.

1435 French defeat English at Gerberoy; the Treaty of Arras between Charles VII and Duke Philippe the Good of Burgundy ends the Anglo-Burgundian alliance.

1436 English evacuate Paris.

1439–40 Praguerie revolt of French nobles.

1441 French retake Pontoise.

1442 French threaten Gascony.

1443 French retake Dieppe.

1444 Truce of Tours; Henry VI agrees to marry Charles VII's niece Margaret of Anjou and relinquish Maine; the Dauphin leads a French army against the Swiss; Charles VII and the Dauphin campaign against *écorcheurs* in Alsace and Lorraine.

1445 Major reforms of the French army.

1448 English garrisons evacuate Maine; English defeated by Scots.

1449 24 March: English seize Fougères in Brittany despite current truce.

1–25 April Rioting in London.

May French take Gerberoy, Cognac, Saint-Mégrin, Conches and Pont-de-l'Arche.

June Charles VII plans reconquest of Normandy; Kentish 'rebels' under Jack Cade reach London.

July Charles VII starts campaign of reconquest in Normandy; rebellion in south-eastern England led by Jack Cade is crushed.

August French take many towns in Normandy; Earl of Douglas defeats English raiding force on Scottish borders.

September–October French take further towns and castles in Normandy, notably Rouen, plus Mauléon in Guyenne.

Late summer to early autumn English send small numbers of reinforcements to Normandy.

October–December English assemble ships from the east coast at Portsmouth, where an army musters under Lord Powis and Sir Thomas Kyriell; French continue to take territory in Normandy and besiege Harfleur.

1450	January: Harfleur and Honfleur surrender to the French; Adam Moleyns is killed by mutinous troops in Southampton.
February	Count of Foix seizes Guiche.
15 March	English army lands at Cherbourg.
16 March	Guillaume de Couvran, Captain of Coutances, sends news of English landing to Charles VII at Alençon.
March (later in month)	English attack Valognes; Duke of Somerset sends reinforcements from Bayeux, Caen and Vire to strengthen Kyriell; Jean de Clermont establishes himself at Carentan.
22 March	French take Fresnay.
10 April	Valognes falls to the English.
12 April	English march towards Bayeux; de Richemont reaches Granville.
13 April	De Richemont reaches Coutances.
14 April	English cross the Grand-Vey and camp at Formigny; de Richemont reaches Saint-Lô.
15 April	French defeat English at battle of Formigny.
23 April (around this date)	French take Vire.
12 May	French take Avranches.
May and early June	Jacques de Luxembourg takes most of the Cotentin peninsula.
16 May	French take Bayeux.
25 June	French take Caen.
21 July	Falaise capitulates to the French.
July (end of month)	Death of Duke François of Brittany.
2 August	Domfront surrenders to French.
22 August	Capitulation of Cherbourg brings Normandy campaign to an end.
October	French invasion of Guyenne begins with siege of Jonsac.
1451	May: Mont-Guyon, Blaye, Bourg, Arqués, Rions, Castillon and Saint-Émilion capitulate to the French.
June	Bordeaux and Fronsac surrender to the French
6 August	French take Bayonne.

1452	
February–March	Yorkist revolt in England ends through negotiation.
August	Charles VII invades Savoy.
June–July	English muster army under Gervase Clifton, Edward Hull and John Talbot.
October	English fleet and army arrive in the Gironde then retake Bordeaux; French rush reinforcements to Blaye.
November–December	English retake Blanquefort, Libourne, Castillon, Rions, Cadillac, Saint-Macaire and Longon but French garrisons retain Fronsac, Blaye and Bourg.
December	Ships assemble at Fowey for the forthcoming expedition to Gascony.
1453	
19 February	English fleet moves to Plymouth.
March	English fleet under John Viscount Lisle sails to Gascony.
March–April	Talbot besieges Fronsac.
2 June	Start of second French campaign to regain Guyenne.
17 July	French defeat English at battle of Castillon.
23 July	Duke of Burgundy defeats army of Ghent at battle of Gavere.
29 July	Châteauneuf and Blanquefort surrender to the French.
August	Henry VI is declared insane.
17 October	Capitulation of Bordeaux concludes campaign in Guyenne.
1455	Beginning of the Wars of the Roses in England.
1457	French fleet attacks Sandwich and Fowey.
1461	Death of Charles VII; he is succeeded by Louis XI.
1475	Truce of Picquigny marks the end of the Hundred Years War.
1558	Calais falls to the French.
1801	English monarchy relinquishes its claim to the throne of France.

OPPOSING FORCES

THE REFORMED FRENCH ARMY OF CHARLES VII

The Truce of Tours in 1444 was not followed by the usual disbandment of most French forces. Instead there was a purging of poor-quality units while the best were retained as a large force under arms. These were now subjected to a thorough process of reform, while continuing to campaign against other enemies. In the same year of the truce with the English, the Dauphin Louis led an army against the Swiss in support of Frederick of Austria and won a notable victory near Basel. The following year Charles VII led a punitive expedition against the city of Metz in support of the Duke of Lorraine and, with his son Louis, dispersed many of the *écorcheurs* (bands of unemployed soldiers) that were terrorizing the region.

The old French army had been raised and organized along much the same lines as the English. Most troops were hired under contract, sometimes as units, sometimes individually, and during the early years of Charles' reign his armies included substantial numbers of foreigners, notably Scots, Spaniards and Italians. From now on, however, the proportion of Frenchmen increased. Nevertheless the Scots are thought to have had a profound influence, especially in the increasing use of mounted-infantry archers and the declining use of crossbows.

Following the siege of Orléans, French armies were also fragmented into smaller companies with little royal control. Even when such forces were not roaming the country, the burden of billeting more military units was unwelcome for most French towns. Not only was it expensive, but the troops were also frequently undisciplined. Indeed it is likely that one purpose of Charles VII's military reforms was to regularize and control such billeting. Ever since the late 14th century soldiers had been subject to widespread criticism, often being portrayed as vain and cowardly and as a source of disorder. In contrast the new, more disciplined troops in direct royal service were widely praised and as a result the differentiation between 'good' and 'bad' soldiers came to be judged in terms of whom they served, 'goodness' being seen as reflecting loyalty to the Crown – a development greatly to the King's benefit.

On 5 January 1445 Charles VII's government formally announced the establishment of royal *compagnies d'ordonnance*, which were regular military formations, largely recruited from the best of the old bands of freelance *écorcheurs*. The rest, many of whom were little better than brigands, were dispersed and, when necessary, crushed. The resulting expensive changes had to be carried out carefully to avoid a revolt by established military captains, some of whom would lose status and earnings even if they avoided dismissal. Indeed it took many years for these reforms to become fully effective and it was Charles VII's grandson, King Charles VIII, who reaped the full benefit (see Campaign 43: *Fornovo 1495*, Osprey Publishing Ltd: Oxford, 1996).

The mid-15th century also witnessed dramatic improvements in guns and gun carriages for field and siege use, though there still seem to have been no real distinctions between the two. Although gunners were still seen as 'dirty artisans' they were no longer regarded as a threat to the established social order. In fact many masters of artillery now came from the minor aristocracy, reflecting the growing prestige of this arm. Fundamental to the improving efficiency of guns was the

Typical French cavalry, preceded by their commander holding his staff of office, in a mid-15th-century copy of the *Legend of Troy*. (Bib. Roy., Ms. 9240, f.23r, Brussels)

development of 'crumbed' gunpowder, which became widespread after 1420. Unlike the original powered form, its constituent elements did not separate during the jolting of transport, and thus was more reliable. The use of separate powder chambers for breech-loading cannon also meant that several such chambers could be prepared in advance, resulting in a remarkably rapid (if brief) rate of fire until these chambers needed refilling. The smaller guns, which were becoming increasingly popular, could also be reloaded and fired faster than the old large-calibre bombards.

The Bureau brothers, Jean and Gaspard, are generally credited with making King Charles VII's artillery such a formidable force. One of their most significant achievements was to regularize the seemingly chaotic variety of battlefield weapons currently in use, as well as purchasing higher-quality and more standardized bronze gun barrels. The resulting weapons still included heavy bombards for siege work, while the veuglair was a smaller-calibre breech-loader. Some cannons also had 'queues' (pig tails), which were a form of swivelled mounting pin that slotted into something fixed and substantial like a wall, parapet or ship's bulwark. The culverin and serpentine were smaller still and were sometimes supported on forks, though neither was a strictly hand-held weapon. Real hand-held guns were also changing as their barrels became longer and thus more accurate, gradually taking over the armour-piercing role of crossbows.

ENGLISH ARMIES IN THE MID-15TH CENTURY

English armies remained small in the mid-15th century, though the cost of their upkeep was a significant burden for the government. Nevertheless, England seems to have had a larger proportion of professional soldiers, vis-à-vis its population, than did France, perhaps reflecting the English government's greater ability to raise money and a willingness to spend a larger percentage of government revenue on warfare. Nevertheless, direct taxation had been

One of the most ambitious of King Charles VII's military reforms in the 1440s was to create the corps of *francs-archers*, an event illustrated in *Martial d'Auvergne's Vigiles de Charles VII*, printed in 1484. (Bib. Nat., Ms. Fr. 5054, f.136, Paris)

bringing in ever-less cash since the mid-14th century; it had slumped since 1430 and had reached a particularly low level in the 1450s. The English Parliament had decided to use the conquered territories in northern France as a source of revenue, but as these slipped from English control so their revenues declined, further undermining attempts to retain those provinces that remained.

Meanwhile, the old system of indenture to recruit troops remained largely unchanged. Indenture contracts had usually been for a period of one year, but in the increasingly difficult financial climate they were often shorter. On the other hand the near panic resulting from the loss of Upper Normandy to the French led to additional incentives being offered to military captains in 1449. The old 'Commission of Array' system remained in place, and although it was intended to raise men to defend their own locality it did provide an administrative structure by which volunteers could be enlisted for campaigns in France.

In England, as in France, the heaviest military burdens fell upon the aristocracy. However, this was a period of remarkable decline and even extinction for many once-noble families. Hence the English government had to recruit new families into the aristocracy to undertake the military and other obligations that went with such status. While the middle classes were undoubtedly on the rise, with many such families joining the aristocracy, it was also a period when the importance of the middle-ranking knightly class increased. Even though higher military command was usually in the hands of the upper nobility, it was not unusual for English field armies to be led by knights. The Formigny campaign is a case in point, though the Castillon campaign is not.

Militarily, the English lands in northern France consisted of the Duchy of Normandy, around which the 'lands of conquest' served as a defensive buffer. Calais was an exception, the port-town being almost entirely inhabited by English settlers while the surrounding 'Pale of Calais' retained its French population, dominated by English garrisons. With the focus of Anglo-French rivalry having been in northern France since the battle of Agincourt, neither side gave much attention to south-western France. Here the frontiers had hardly changed and the English administration had done little to solve the old problem of feudal relations between the Plantagenet Duchy of Aquitaine and the French Crown.

ABOVE
A mid-15th-century breech-loading veuglair cannon was found in Lisieux Castle. (Musée des Antiquités, Rouen; author's photograph)

BOTTOM
A copy of a French translation of Livy's *History of Rome*, printed in the middle of the 15th century, showing soldiers and fortifications from the period. (*Tite-Live*, Bib. Nat., Ms. Fr. 33, f.233v, Paris)

Feudal obligations within this 'English France' remained traditional, with the English authorities in Normandy never abandoning the belief that the local aristocracy owed them military service. A large number of Norman lords had, however, been dispossessed because they refused to recognize the English King's claim to the French Crown, most such families then moving to 'French France' as staunch supporters of King Charles VII. Their lands were then taken by large numbers of noblemen of English origin, many of whom also held lands in England. Yet even they declined as a reliable source of troops after 1436. Meanwhile, there was increasing doubt about the reliability of the local Norman troops who supposedly defended Normandy's fortified towns and cities, despite threats of harsh punishment if they failed in their duties.

In complete contrast, Gascon lords, knights, soldiers and militias remained loyal to their distant English king and often seemed keener to fight the French than the English garrisons were. Under King Henry VI, Gascons were, in fact, given greater responsibility for local defence than they had had since the late 14th century, while the English tended to send significant military contingents only in times of crisis.

Both Normandy, the 'lands of conquest' and Gascony were nevertheless strongly garrisoned and these garrisons, like the English field armies in France, included men from a remarkable variety of backgrounds; not only Englishmen and Normans but also Gascons, Bretons, Frenchmen, Irishmen, Germans, Spaniards, Lombards and Dutchmen. There were also many cases when men changed sides, Pierre de Brézé being an example. But as the English position weakened, so it became harder to recruit men for what looked like a lost cause. Thus the proportion of Englishmen increased, though they did not necessarily prove any more reliable.

While financial constraints in England reduced the size of garrisons in France, they also led to most English expeditionary forces being significantly

smaller than those of the 14th century. The proportion of various types of troops similarly varied, those with a larger number of archers being easier to raise in a time of crisis, cheaper, and more suitable if the expedition intended to attack a castle or relieve one already under siege.[1]

Despite mounting problems, English armies in France remained highly effective and mobile but seemingly clung to the traditional strategy of devastating *chevauchée* raids to inflict economic damage on enemy territory and to bring enemy forces into battle, where the English archers retained a tradition of victory. These forces were much less suitable for a long-term occupation, or for fighting the sort of defensive war that the French now imposed. Worse still, if men were withdrawn from garrisons to fill the ranks of field armies, the places they had been defending became vulnerable. Consequently, the bulk of field forces had to be sent from England as and when needed.

Whereas the French put great effort into modernizing their tactics and troops, the English clung to a conservative faith in the primacy of the English archer. English military literature of this period also tended to be highly traditional if not downright archaic. However, where guns were concerned, England differed from France in that gunpowder artillery remained firmly under government control, despite the retinues of major lords and military leaders including artillerymen and related specialists. The English also put a great deal of effort and money into the fortifications of Normandy, especially those of major towns, with a total of no less than 170 garrisoned locations being recorded. Similarly, in Aquitaine and Gascony, which had been strongly fortified over many centuries, the English administration continued to modernize the defences.

Naval warfare was clearly more important to England than to France, being essential for communications and to transport its armies. In fact during the 15th century it was generally accepted that the English were, in the words of the heralds of this period, *roys de la mer*. Nevertheless the French soon had control of most of the best ports and also seem to have developed superior capabilities in ship construction, while the English naval effort may still have been hampered by long-standing and traditional hostility between the sailors of East Anglia on the North Sea coast and those of the Cinque Ports farther south.

The English Admiralty seal of John Holland, made between 1435 and 1442. The ship is distorted to fit the shape of the seal but nevertheless represents a typical armed transport vessel of the period. (National Maritime Museum, London)

MORALE AND THE RISE OF NATIONALISM

For many years it was accepted that the Hundred Years War stimulated the rise of the nation state in England and France. More recently this simplistic interpretation has been challenged, with greater emphasis being given to the role the huge costs of warfare played in the centralization of military, political and economic power. Yet this still leaves the Hundred Years War as a major factor.

Then there was the cultural impact of this conflict, especially in England, where there was a clear link with the rise of English rather than French as the language of literature and government. Although the process started before the Hundred Years War, it remained hesitant until the 15th century. But by then there was a contrary feeling of war-weariness, and nostalgia for past glories and victory was overtaken by reality.

---

1 Curry, A., 'English Armies in the Fifteenth Century' in A. Curry and M. Hughes (eds.), *Arms, Armies and Fortifications in the Hundred Years War* (Woodbridge, 1994) pp. 45–47.

LEFT
France and England imported large quantities of armour from both Germany and Italy during the 15th century, the German style being shown in this panel painting of the warriors Sibbechai and Benaja by Konrad Witz, *c*.1445. (Kunstmuseum, Basel)

RIGHT
Despite increasing political chaos, England remained remarkably prosperous, and its churches often contained vigorous carvings like this 15th-century pew end showing sleeping guards at the Holy Sepulchre. (*In situ* Church of St John the Baptist, Hatch Beauchamp; author's photograph)

Attitudes in France changed in rather different ways, and it was perhaps here that proto-nationalist ideas first took root. Rather than relying on older concepts of 'just war', the legal profession began using seemingly modern ideas such as 'France for the French and England for the English'. Meanwhile, the French king increasingly felt it necessary to appeal to French public opinion as well as to the traditional loyalty of the military classes. Indeed, by the mid-15th century it was generally accepted that as the 'true king', Charles VII should be supported by all 'true Frenchmen', although such ideas faced more resistance amongst the nobility than lower down the social scale.

Until recently, French historians have emphasized the local resistance to English rule in Normandy and the 'lands of conquest', whereas English historians have tended to dismiss this as a response to excessive taxation. As usual the reality lies somewhere in between, and there were also variations in the degree of pro- or anti-English sentiment, especially amongst lesser lords, who switched sides more easily than did those higher up the aristocratic hierarchy. A significant proportion of the Norman church was also notably pro-English, perhaps fearing domination by the clerical hierarchy in Paris. The attitudes of the urban merchant and artisan classes were more parochial, largely being concerned with good governance and law and order, which would permit trade to flourish.

The situation in south-western France was different. Here pro-English sentiment ran deep, and some noble families had centuries-old traditions of supporting the English authorities in Bordeaux. Meanwhile, in a region seemingly dominated by the complex relationships and loyalties of the Gascon nobility, the attitudes of lesser folk tend to get ignored. Nevertheless, pro-English sentiment in cities like Bordeaux was based upon sound commercial self-interest as well as tradition. It might also be significant that the University of Bordeaux was founded under English rule in 1442 to enable youngsters from the Gascon elite to receive an education without leaving their native land – more specifically without having to go to Paris.

OPPOSING COMMANDERS

FRENCH COMMANDERS

Although **King Charles VII** did not personally take part in the battles of Formigny or Castillon, he led the invasion that resulted in the former battle and was in active command of one of the armies that invaded English-ruled Gascony in 1453. Initially, Charles was seen as a weak-willed man but he came to be seen as one of the most effective and wisest rulers in French history. Indeed his reign was regarded as 'a time of marvels'.

As King, Charles VII overcame a deep abhorrence of war, at least of its planning and logistical organization, yet he was never timid in his relations with strong women, ranging from Jeanne d'Arc to his mistress Agnes Sorel. The *Tale of La Belle Agnes* became very popular in France, telling how the love of a beautiful woman from the middle ranks of the French aristocracy transformed the lethargic Charles VII into a valiant king.

Jean de Clermont, came from the uppermost echelons of French society but was still young when he was nominal commander of the French army at Formigny. He had not yet even been knighted (this ceremony being carried

LEFT
Charles VII attended by senior military commanders, including Arthur de Richemont, the Bureau brothers and Joachim Rouault, in a 15th-century French manuscript. (Rouen, Bib. Munic., Ms. 1151)

RIGHT
The 'Allegory of Blind Death' made for de Clermont, whose coat of arms appears below the picture. (Bib. Nat., Ms. Fr. 1989, f.34, Paris)

out after the victory). Jean's father was Charles I de Bourbon, a generally loyal supporter of Charles VII who had nevertheless been involved in the Praguerie revolt of nobles in 1440. Jean's military career nevertheless earned him the nickname 'Scourge of the English', while his later years earned him the name 'Jean the Good' despite quarrelling with the King as his father had done before him. During his long and eventful life, Jean also showed himself to be a cultured man, supporting the poet François Villon and creating a great library and a remarkable zoological garden in his castle of Moulins.

Arthur III de Richemont was one of three constables of France who came from Brittany during the Hundred Years War. Born in 1393, a younger son of Duke Jean V of Brittany, he was made titular Earl of Richmond in England by the Duke of Bedford in 1414 (hence his name). He also inherited the titles of Duke of Brittany and Count of Montfort from his nephew Duke Peter II, but died less than a year later in 1458.

Arthur de Richemont's fame, of course, rests on his remarkable military career. It was certainly eventful; he supported the Armagnacs against the Burgundians during the French civil war in 1410–14, was wounded and captured at the battle of Agincourt and then released in 1420. Four years later, and with the English title of 'Count of Richmond', Arthur returned to Charles' allegiance and was made constable of the so-called 'Kingdom of Bourges'. As an enthusiastic supporter of Jeanne d'Arc, de Richemont fought by her side against the English at the battle of Patay. Later, he smoothed the way for the vital alliance between France and Burgundy, after which his role as constable placed him in the forefront of the final campaigns against the English. As a result, like most people in this role, de Richemont spent most of his working life on the move around France, these journeys being well recorded in several sources.[2]

Jean V de Bueil is remembered as much for his book *Le Jouvencel* as for his role as a commander. Born in 1406, the son of Jean IV de Bueil who was killed at the battle of Agincourt and grandson of Jean III who had fought against John of Gaunt's Great Chevauchée in 1373 (see Campaign 9:

2 Kerhervé, J., 'Une existance en perpétuel mouvement, Arthur de Richement…' in (anon. ed.), *Viajeros, peregrinos, mercaderes en el Occidente Medieval, XIII Semana de Estudios Medievales, Estella, 22 a 26 Julio de 1991* (Pamplona, 1992) pp. 109–12.

Agincourt 1415, Osprey Publishing Ltd: Oxford, 1991, and Raid 20: *The Great Chevauchée*, Osprey Publishing Ltd: Oxford, 2011), Jean V earned the nickname '*Fléau des Anglais*' ('Scourge of the English'). As Captain of Tours in 1426, then Captain General of Anjou and Maine and Admiral of France in August 1450, Jean V fought in several major battles; he and Jacques de Chabannes both claimed credit for victory at Castillon. *Le Jouvencel* was written a decade or so before Jean V's death in 1477 and is a semi-autobiographical account of the latter part of the Hundred Years War, told through the mouth of a fictitious military hero.

Jean Bureau was born around 1390 in the Champagne region of France, though his parents were merchants from Paris. The family then moved back to the French capital, where Jean studied law before being employed by the English governing regime. In 1434 he left Paris to offer his services to King Charles VII, where he was described as 'a citizen of Paris, a man of small stature but of purpose and daring, particularly skilled and experienced in the use of artillery'. He eventually became 'governor of the French archers', and his brother Gaspard Bureau became 'master of ordnance'. Nevertheless, Jean himself was Master Gunner of French Artillery in 1439, eventually being entrusted by Charles VII with most of the final siege operations in Normandy and Gascony. This brought considerable prestige to the Bureau brothers, and as a result Jean was made Treasurer of France and Mayor of Bordeaux once it was back in French hands. Jean was also knighted in 1461. Of course, the Bureau brothers were viewed differently from the English side, and this is still reflected in some modern works; M. B. Christie describes Jean Bureau as the 'evil genius' of the French campaigns.

ENGLISH COMMANDERS

Edmund Beaufort, Duke of Somerset, was in overall command as the Lieutenant of English Normandy at the time of its collapse, and his reputation has suffered as a result. Born in 1406, a grandson of John of Gaunt and Katherine Swynford, the fact that Edmund Beaufort was from one of the greatest families in England did not mean that he was particularly rich. In fact, his shortage of money caused him considerable political difficulties. Nevertheless, Edmund's wide military experience brought him command of a moderately successful English army in 1431. He later served as Lieutenant of English Normandy in France and replaced his political rival, the Duke of York, as military commander in 1448. However, the loss of Normandy left Edmund vulnerable to those who supported the opposing Yorkist cause. Edmund was a dominant figure at the start of the Wars of the Roses, but was killed in the first battle of St Albans in 1455.

Sir Thomas Kyriell came from a family of what might be called 'middle-ranking knights'. Their original Norman-French name was 'De Criol', and they had served as sheriffs and in other comparable roles for at least two centuries. Around 1343 the Kyriell family built much of the existing castle of Westenhanger near Folkstone in Kent, where Thomas was probably brought up. Thomas Kyriell himself was a Knight of the Garter and he fought with distinction in France, often alongside John Talbot, and most notably in the Picardy coastal region in the late 1430s. Thomas was clearly respected by his French opponents, and some of the most detailed information about his career is found in French chronicles.

TOP
Henry VI of England giving a sword to John Talbot in the *Shrewsbury Book*, a collection of chivalric romances given to Queen Margaret by Talbot in 1445. (Brit. Lib., Royal Ms. E.VI, f.405)

RIGHT
The castle of Westenhanger in Kent was the family home of the Kyriell family. It was presumably here that Thomas Kyriell grew up and perhaps received his first military training. (Ian Knox photograph)

Nevertheless, Kyriell had defeats as well as victories. He and his future co-commander at Formigny, Matthew Gough, suffered a severe setback at the Bridge of Meulan in 1453, where Gough was captured. Thomas also found himself in trouble as Captain of Calais, where there was such difficulty paying the troops that the governor feared that these disgruntled men would seize the valuable stores of wool that formed the mainstay of Calais's trade. Worse still, Thomas was suspected of illegal profiteering and his reputation was already tarnished by the mid-1440s when, as Captain of Gisors, he was accused of stealing the soldiers' wages. After being released following his capture at the battle of Formigny, he became a Member of Parliament and was one of those who supported the Yorkists in their political opposition to Edmund Beaufort. Thomas was captured at the second battle of St Albans in 1461 and was one of the senior prisoners whom Queen Margaret brought before her young son, demanding that he condemn the men to death. Thomas called down a curse upon the Queen's head for teaching her child such cruelty, and was summarily executed.

John Talbot was born between 1384 and 1387, a descendant of Sir Gilbert Talbot, who had been King Edward III's lord chamberlain in 1331. In 1407 John married a woman from the powerful Nevill family, while his second marriage was to an heiress of the wealthy Beauchamp family. His first military experience was against Welsh rebels, after which he served as Lord Lieutenant of Ireland, earning a reputation for harshness. However, it was in France that he earned the fame that has made him into a somewhat undeservedly archetypal English hero.

After missing the great English victory at Agincourt, Talbot returned to Ireland, but was back in France in time to be captured at the battle of Patay. Exchanged for a famous French commander, Jean Poton de Xaintrailles, he and Thomas Kyriell found themselves facing Xaintrailles and La Hire near the town of Ry in Normandy in 1436, where the English were victorious. Like so many military leaders during this period, John knew failure and success. Although none of his victories rated as major battles, his reputation was such that he was made Earl of Shrewsbury in 1442. Popularly believed to have been 80 years old when he was killed outside Castillon in 1453, he was actually closer to 70, which was still very old for a medieval battlefield commander.

Almost a hundred years after John Talbot's death the English chronicler Edward Hall wrote of him: 'This man was to the French people, a very scourge and daily terror, in so much as that his person was fearful and terrible to his adversaries present, so his name and fame was spiteful and dreadful to the common people absent, in so much that women in France to fear their young children would cry "the Talbot cometh, the Talbot cometh".'[3]

---

3 Pollard, A. J., *John Talbot and the War in France, 1427–1453* (London, 1983) p. 2.

THE FALL OF NORMANDY

When King Henry VI's government moved to hand Maine over to the French, as had been secretly agreed in December 1445, it faced strong resistance from many of the English and their supporters, who feared that further territory might be surrendered if French pressure was not resisted. The garrison in Le Mans refused to leave and so, in November 1447, the French threatened to renew hostilities. That same year war broke out yet again between England and Scotland. The weakness of King Henry VI's position was clear to all, and his policy of seeking peace at almost any cost disintegrated. Four months later the garrison in Le Mans realized that they had no alternative and so withdrew from Maine, further weakening England's strategic position in Normandy.

Not all the English forces in Normandy were willing to accept this new reality, and on 24 March 1449 François de Surienne, the Captain of Verneuil and in English service, attacked the Breton fortress of Fougères, probably with the acquiescence of the Duke of Suffolk, the power behind the throne in England. The unsuspecting Breton town was pillaged, much to the embarrassment of Arthur de Richemont who was supposedly responsible for its safety. His nephew, Duke François I of Brittany, who had previously avoided committing himself too firmly to one side or the other, appealed to Charles VII of France for help. Meanwhile, Edmund Beaufort refused even to offer an apology, and so the French retaliated by seizing Pont-de-l'Arche, Gerberoy and Conches in Normandy, while Cognac and Saint-Mégrin in the south-west were also taken in May. When Beaufort refused an offer to exchange Fougères for these towns, Charles VII declared war at the end of July 1449. This came at a very bad time for the English government, with serious disorder in some parts of the country and deep dissatisfaction almost everywhere. In addition, on 12 August the Earl of Douglas defeated an English force on the Scottish borders.

A well-coordinated assault by Charles VII and François I now reconquered much of Normandy in less than a year, largely because the English were hopelessly unprepared but also because the majority of the Norman population supported the French cause. Although the Duke of Burgundy was preoccupied with a rebellion in Flanders, the French were reportedly strengthened by some Burgundian troops while several French *compagnies* were redeployed from peacetime locations in the south, including some of Charles VII's foreign forces.

This French campaign was conducted by four separate armies, the first success being achieved by Pierre de Brézé, who seized the vital town of Verneuil on 19 July 1449. The place was supposedly betrayed by a local militiaman whom the English had beaten for sleeping at his post. On 6 August King Charles VII himself crossed the river Loire to take command, eventually joining forces with the army led by Jean de Dunois. On 8 August the French took Pont-Audemer and hardly a week then seemed to pass without another major English-held town or castle falling. On 26 August the inhabitants of Mantes forced the English garrison to surrender by seizing control of a tower and gate. Around the same time, Roche-Guyon was reportedly surrendered by its captain in exchange for an assurance that he could keep the lands of his French wife. In September, the Duke of Brittany formally handed over to King Charles VII's representative all those places the Breton army had captured in western Normandy. Meanwhile, in southern Normandy the Duke of Alençon seized the major fortified city of Alençon, which had been beyond his control for decades.

On 13 October there was a procession of children through Paris to give thanks for these astonishing victories, though the campaign was certainly not over. Three days later Charles VII and Dunois besieged the Norman capital of Rouen, which fell in less than a week. Here the English fought hard but not for long, the inhabitants being divided, some sending a deputation to England begging for support while others insisting that the garrison surrender. Edmund Beaufort was in overall command and agreed to negotiate. Realizing that no help could arrive from England in time, he agreed to surrender. His more belligerent subordinate, Talbot, was one of eight hostages handed over to the French while Beaufort and the garrison were allowed to march to English-held Caen.

Eventually, on 10 November 1449, King Charles VII made his ceremonial entry into Rouen. A little under a fortnight later the massive Château-Gaillard, key to navigation along the river Seine between Paris and the coast, surrendered to the French, and Fougères was retaken by the Duke of Brittany. In the light of this unfolding disaster, Queen Margaret and the Duke of Suffolk, the most powerful figures in England, decided to make a major military effort, raising a substantial army in the latter part of 1449. A fleet also had to be gathered to transport the 4,500 retained men to Normandy, but it was already late autumn by the time ships 'arrested' on the eastern coasts of England assembled at Portsmouth, where the troops were mustered.

The fighting men had been retained for an initial period of three months, and were now placed under the command of Lord Powis and Sir Thomas Kyriell, the most experienced commander currently available. Even before this new army could sail, the English outposts in Normandy needed food and supplies from southern England, where defeated English soldiers and loyalist Frenchmen from Normandy were already becoming a nuisance. Eventually, restrictions were imposed around some Channel ports and the displaced men were forced to 'go home'. The assembled army at Portsmouth then learned

For centuries, Valognes was strategically vital for control of the Cotentin Peninsula, changing hands several times during 1449 and 1450. Its fine Gothic church was badly damaged on 21 June 1944 during the battle of Normandy. (Author's photograph)

The first phase of the French reconquest of Normandy 1449–50

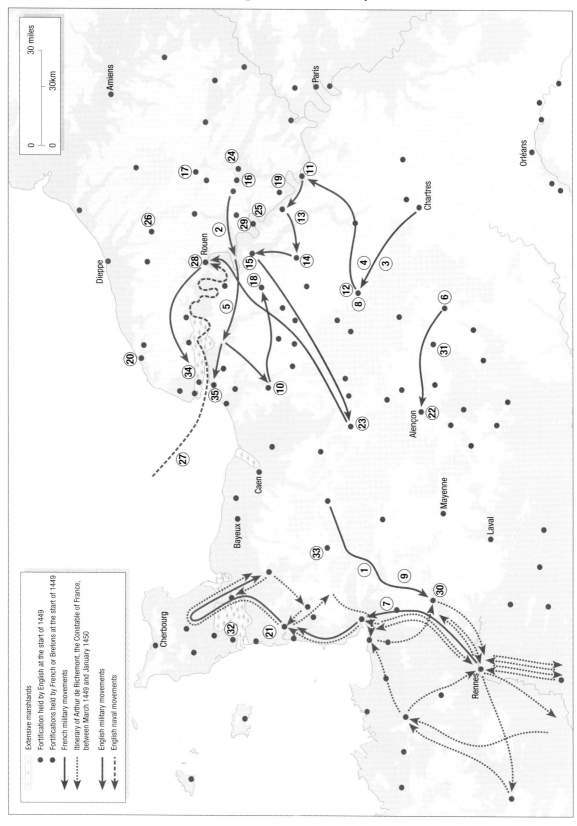

that the second instalment of their pay would be delayed until March 1450, and on 9 January a group of disgruntled soldiers and sailors assaulted Adam Moleyns, the Keeper of the Privy Seal, before one of their captains, Cuthbert Colville, killed the unfortunate Moleyns. The Duke of Suffolk was widely regarded as responsible for the defeats. As a result he was eventually arrested and impeached by Parliament. Although the Duke of Suffolk was found to be not guilty, he nevertheless thought it advisable to leave the country; he did not get far, being assassinated as he sailed for Normandy on 3 May 1450.

Meanwhile, the winter of 1449–50 saw the English position in Normandy growing ever more desperate, where Edmund Beaufort was so short of money that he had to send some troops home. Others simply deserted. Things looked better for the English in Gascony, but even here the Count of Foix seized Guichen near Bayonne in February 1450. Such was the French determination to retake Normandy that hostilities continued through the winter. An effort to surprise La Haye-du-Puits in December was defeated, but a few days later the French had their revenge when Geoffroy de Couvran and Joachim Rouault defeated the English garrison of Vire outside their town.

1 English seize Breton fortress of Fougères despite a truce, 24 March 1449.
2 French retaliate by taking Pont-de-l'Arche, 15 May 1449.
3 Pierre de Brézé attacks Verneuil, 19 July 1449.
4 Charles VII crosses river Loire to take command of French southern army, 6 August 1449.
5 French northern army seizes Pont-Audemer, 8 August 1449.
6 French besiege and take Nogent-Pré, 8–9 August 1449.
7 Saint-James-de-Beuvron surrenders.
8 Verneuil surrenders, 25 August 1449.
9 Saint-Guillaume-de-Mortain falls, 25 August 1449.
10 Lisieux falls around 25 August 1449.
11 Mantes surrenders, 26 August 1449.
12 Ceremonial entry of Charles VII into Verneuil, 27 August 1449.
13 Siege and capitulation of Vernon, 28–30 August 1449.
14 Charles VII is ceremonially received by the garrison of Evreux, end of August 1449.
15 Louviers opens its gates to Charles VII, end of August 1449.
16 Dangu falls, end of August 1449.
17 Gournay falls, end of August 1449.
18 Harcourt falls, end of August 1449.
19 Roche-Guyon falls, late August or early September 1449.
20 Fécamp falls, September 1449.
21 Bretons besiege Avranches and take most of the Cotentin Peninsula and Saint-Lô, August and early September 1449.
22 Duke of Alençon retakes Alençon, September 1449.
23 French southern army takes Argentan, late September 1449.
24 Gisors falls, end of September 1449.
25 French besiege Château-Gaillard, end of September 1449.
26 French take Neufchâtel-en-Bray, September–October 1449.
27 Small numbers of English reinforcements sent to Normandy, late summer and early autumn 1449.
28 French besiege and take Rouen, 16–22 October 1449; Charles VII makes a ceremonial entry into the city on 10 November 1449.
29 Château-Gaillard surrenders, 23 November 1449.
30 English garrison in Fougères surrenders, 23 November 1449.
31 Bellême surrenders, end of November 1449.
32 Unsuccessful Franco-Breton attempt to seize La Haye-du-Puits, December 1449.
33 Franco-Breton ambush English garrison of Vire, December 1449.
34 French besiege and take Harfleur, 8 December 1449 to 1 January 1450.
35 French besiege and take Honfleur, 17–18 January 1450.

In the Middle Ages the strategically located town of Carentan stood on an island surrounded by extensive marshes, and it controlled the main crossing point between the eastern part of the Cotentin Peninsula and the rest of Normandy. (Author's photograph)

The most important of these winter operations was against the port of Harfleur. A siege began on 8 December and, under King Charles VII's supervision, was pressed hard despite freezing conditions until the English garrison capitulated on 1 January 1450. Less than three weeks later, Honfleur, on the other side of the Seine estuary, also fell. Yet these victories resulted in a personal tragedy for King Charles VII, his beloved mistress Agnes Sorel dying at Jumièges after travelling in deep winter to visit Charles at the siege of Harfleur.

THE ENGLISH INVASION

Despite such disasters, the English still held the central part of western Normandy centred upon the strongly garrisoned cities of Caen (which was under imminent threat from Charles VII's army) and Bayeux, plus Falaise and part of the Cotentin peninsula including Cherbourg. The latter was the only major harbour that the English now controlled, and it enabled them to bring in supplies. Almost as soon as weather permitted, the new English army set sail and landed at Cherbourg on 15 March 1450. Something over 100 years later the chronicler Richard Grafton wrote: 'The king of England sent into Normandie… a valiant Capteyn called sir Thomas Kiriell: a man of great stomack, if he had a great army, but his power was to small, either to recover that which was lost, either to save that which yet remayned ungotten'.

Kyriell's arrival raised English morale in Normandy and his orders seem to have been to support Bayeux, but as the French now held key castles in the Cotentin Peninsula he could not set out immediately. In particular, French-held Valognes would threaten his communication so this became his first target. Edmund Beaufort agreed and sent Kyriell troops from the remaining English garrisons in Normandy, consisting of 600 men under Robert Vere from Caen, 800 under Matthew Gough from Bayeux and about 400 under Henry Norberry from Vire.

Meanwhile, the vulnerable French garrison at Valognes was currently under the command of a squire, Abel Rouault, during the absence of its captain, his brother Joachim Rouault. Abel sent urgent requests for support to de Richemont and other French commanders, but Kyriell moved too fast, attacking Valognes within days of landing. The garrison held out for three weeks before capitulating on 10 April. Whether the arrival of the reinforcements sent by Edmund Beaufort convinced Abel Rouault to submit is unclear, but he was allowed to depart with his men, together with their goods, horses and possessions.

The Cotentin Peninsula was a fertile part of Normandy in which the English army could organize itself before marching across enemy territory, initially to Bayeux but then towards Caen, which feared an imminent French attack. To do this, however, they had either to take or somehow bypass Carentan, which controlled the main road and which was itself held by de Clermont. Kyriell decided on the latter course, leading his army across the difficult coastal marshes and estuaries of the Grand-Vey. Abel Rouault's defiance at Valognes had cost them valuable time but, two days after the fall of Valognes, the English set out.

The French had not, of course, been idle. At the time Kyriell was landing at Cherbourg, Arthur de Richemont had been near Redon in southern Brittany while Duke François of Brittany was at Dinan in the north, and had reportedly wanted to move against the invaders immediately. However, he was dissuaded by his council, perhaps giving way because he was in the midst

TOP
Le Porte at Brevands, looking upriver. Between Carentan and the English Channel the tidal estuary was flanked by extensive marshes in the 15th century while a few kilometres to the east lay the similar estuary of the Vire. (Author's photograph)

BOTTOM
Looking north across the medieval main road from Carentan to Bayeaux, towards the village of Formigny. (Author's photograph)

of a political crisis after imprisoning his brother and designated heir, Gilles de Bretagne, who was strongly in favour of an alliance with the English. On 25 April François would order that Gilles be strangled by his gaolers, but in the meantime the Duke had reservations about letting his recently re-formed Breton army get involved in the forthcoming campaign. In contrast, Arthur de Richemont was much more enthusiastic, both about the alliance with Charles VII and about fighting the English.

Meanwhile, French commanders were acutely aware of the danger of the army under Kyriell and the garrisons under Somerset joining forces. They were of course fully informed of English movements. Only a day after the English had landed at Cherbourg, Guillaume de Couvran, the French Captain of Coutances, sent a messenger to Alençon to inform Charles VII. He in turn informed the commander of the French army in this area, the young Count Jean de Clermont, who soon had some of the most famous captains in France under his command. Nevertheless this elite force remained small in numbers – a mere 500–600 lances (a lance contained three to five men) plus some mounted archers. Unable to save Valognes, de Clermont instead established himself in Carentan, and while Geoffroy de Couvran and Joachim Rouault watched the enemy's march, de Clermont asked Arthur de Richemont to hurry to defend Saint-Lô. De Richemont was at Countances when he received de Clermont's letters, and promptly set off via Perriers and La Haye-du-Puits with an army that was even smaller than that headed by de Clermont.

Meanwhile, to the south-east, the French took the isolated enemy outpost at Fresnay-sur-Sarthe on 22 March. The English plan was to assemble troops from as many garrisons as possible in order to form an army large enough to roll back the French gains. While Kyriell's force was relatively lightly equipped, some of these garrisons had substantial siege trains, including artillery, and, according to the chronicler Thomas Basin, in Caen Edmund Beaufort, 'had placed on carts bombards, mangonels and other war machines'.

FROM THE GRAND-VEY TO FORMIGNY

Once it became clear that Kyriell was neither heading for Saint-Lô nor intending to attack Carentan, Jean de Clermont 'took council' on the best way of attacking the enemy. Some noted that the English would be vulnerable as they crossed the Grand-Vey. Others advised attacking the enemy from the rear on the firm ground in the Bessin area further east, and this was what Jean de Clermont decided.

The crossing of the Grand-Vey was nevertheless a remarkable feat by Kyriell's army. The area consisted of a broad bay, which included vast areas of tidal sands backed by extensive sand dunes pierced by the Carentan and Isigny rivers. These rivers could be crossed at two fords, 5km apart and called the Fords of Saint-Clément. Unless the crossing was carefully planned, the English were in as much danger from the tide as from the French, the marsh and sands extending for 6–7km in front of the two fords. Then there is the question of how long it would take a narrow column of at least 6,000 men plus their horses and baggage animals to cross. As it happened, the crossing date of 14 April could hardly have been better, with a new moon the following day ensuring that the beach between the fords was uncovered for five or even six hours.[4]

4 Trévédy, J-T-M., 'La Bataille de Formigny (15 April 1450)' in *Bulletin de la Société Archéologique de Finisterre*, 30 (1903) pp. 269–73.

Despite Jean de Clermont's orders, many local people insisted on trying to prevent the English from crossing, even accusing their own leaders of treason for not doing the same. When local men, farmers and archers assembled from Carentan and nearby villages, de Clermont felt obliged to send a company of men-at-arms to help but, not surprisingly, the English brushed such uncoordinated resistance aside, Matthew Gough reportedly shouting at the French: 'Mad dogs! We crossed despite you!'

Kyriell and Gough then led their army to the village of Formigny and made camp for the night. Why they did not press on to Bayeux is unknown, as the troops had not marched very far. Gough was then sent on to Bayeux, perhaps seeking reinforcements for a planned ambush of the pursuing force under de Clermont. French plans are much clearer, with de Clermont now deciding to attack the English the following day. He therefore sent the parish priest of Carentan to inform de Richemont, urging him to march to Trévières and attack the English flank. De Clermont's army therefore set off the following morning with Odet d'Aidie in charge of the scouts, followed by Admiral Prigent de Coëtivy with the vanguard.

De Richemont received de Clermont's message around dawn on the 15th, but his army was not ready to march at such short notice. So he took Mass, before setting off for Trévières with only six men. A few kilometres down the road he stopped in an area of open countryside, where it was easier to array his army. Once that was done, he sent the Bastard of La Trémoille ahead with 15 or 20 lances as scouts, followed by the vanguard under the Marshal de Lohéac, Jacques de Luxembourg and Jean II de Brosse. Next came Gilles de Saint-Simon, Jean and Philippe de Malestroit with the mounted archers and then de Richemont himself with the rest of the army, which is said to have totalled between 200 and 240 lances plus 800 archers.

THE BATTLE OF FORMIGNY

There is still considerable disagreement about the size of the armies at the battle of Formigny. Ferdinand Lot, for example, calculated that the English outnumbered de Clermont's army by some two-to-one, and that even after de Richemont arrived the English still had a numerical advantage. In contrast, the English chroniclers and more recent historians seem unable to accept that the English were defeated by a smaller French force.

LEFT
Until recently, part of the old road just west of Formigny remained unmodernized. Though a 19th-century *grande route*, it was similar to the medieval main road that formed the main east–west artery across this part of Normandy. (Author's photograph)

RIGHT
There was probably a watermill on the site of the Moulin de la Bretonnière, just outside the village of Normanville, at the time of the nearby battle of Formigny. (Author's photograph)

At the start of the battle the English also had the huge advantage of holding a strong defensive position, though this would be negated by the arrival of the second, albeit small, French army. The fact that Gough was hurriedly recalled from the road to Bayeux also suggests that de Clermont arrived from the west faster than Kyriell had expected, though the English continued erecting the field fortifications they had seemingly been working on all morning. These consisted of large potholes and ditches, which the English excavated in front of their position, also planting sharpened stakes in the ground and strengthening the walls, hedges, gardens and orchards of the village as a hindrance to cavalry. Furthermore, the English protected their rear with some sort of smaller field fortification east of Formigny and probably posted a guard at the bridge over the river Aure on the road to Bayeux.

The English array at the start of the battle consisted of two elements, the larger one on the right being under Kyriell's command and drawn up next to the village. The smaller one on the left was under Gough, who had now returned to Formigny, and was closer to the Val stream. Most of the English army, including the archers, was now dismounted, although Kyriell may have posted cavalry to defend the bridge across the Val. Gough's men also seem to have been placed on both sides of the road and were the first to be engaged.

De Clermont's army arrived shortly after midday, with part of its vanguard consisting of the Scottish *compagnie* under Cunningham. As the English scouts withdrew, de Clermont's men approached the Val stream but stopped beyond the range of the English archers. The two sides then observed each other for another three hours. Next, de Clermont sent some gunners forward with two light cannon to bombard Gough's men, the gunners under Louis Giribault being protected by dismounted archers and 50–60 lances of men-at-arms under Floquet and the Sire of Mauny. De Clermont was now receiving conflicting advice, the older commanders advising restraint while the younger ones were urging an assault before the English field fortifications grew any stronger.

By standing for so long on the defensive, the English offered an easy target for the guns and, although there were only two in action, they caused sufficient casualties for 500–600 of Gough's archers to make an apparently unauthorized attack across the bridge, driving off the gunners and those protecting them and capturing the two cannon. It was apparently at this point that a unit of men-at-arms under Pierre de Brézé charged in support of their discomforted comrades. A bitter struggle ensued, with the English archers being reinforced

This remarkable 15th-century drawing shows Constable Arthur de Richemont (upper right) greeting Jean de Clermont (upper left) when their armies combined at the battle of Formigny. (*Memoire de Peiresc*, Bib. Nat., Ms. Nouv. Acq. Fr. 5174, f.41, Paris)

by men sent by Kyriell. According to Coëtivy, writing an official report four days after the battle, if the English had now launched a full-scale offensive, de Clermont's army would have been in serious trouble.

Although Kyriell and Gough did not attack, de Clermont sent local peasants to look for de Richemont somewhere to the south. By the time de Richemont crossed the river Aure the battle had already been going on for several hours. After climbing the slope to the plateau, he arrayed his army for battle and a local tradition maintains that he climbed a windmill to see what was happening. Whether or not the English had observers near Trévières, they became rapidly aware of the newcomers, shouting in triumph in the belief that they were reinforcements. Quite why reinforcements should arrive from the south remains unknown, and the English were soon disabused, recognizing French banners and realizing that they were in danger of being outflanked.

De Clermont was probably aware of de Richemont's arrival before the English were, though perhaps not much before, for he now sent men to retake the guns before they could be dragged across the bridge. From that point onwards accounts of the battle become very confused. Pierre de Brézé seemingly led this charge by men-at-arms on foot, regaining the guns and, according to Chartier, driving the English back and killing some 200 of them. The English army was now attempting to wheel its left wing more than 90 degrees in order to defend the village of Formigny. Gough's men had by far the greatest distance to move and in all likelihood this hugely ambitious redeployment could have succeeded only if the French had not intervened.

Unfortunately for the English, de Clermont and de Richemont seized the moment, the latter having hurried to confer with de Clermont while sending

JEAN DE CLERMONT AND ARTHUR DE RICHEMONT MEET ON THE BATTLEFIELD OF FORMIGNY, MID-AFTERNOON, 15 APRIL 1450 (pp. 32–33)

The battle of Formigny was rare in the history of medieval European warfare because two small and separate armies succeeded in linking up while fighting was actually taking place and, by coordinating their actions, they defeated an enemy force that was larger than either of them. Even when combined, the French armies may not have been larger than the English force facing them. One French army was commanded by the still relatively inexperienced Jean de Clermont, and the other by Arthur de Richemont, the highly experienced Constable of France. On the other side the English were led by two battle-hardened professional soldiers, Thomas Kyriell and Matthew Gough. Furthermore, English troops were hugely confident in their own superiority whereas the French, despite several decades of success against English invaders, remained somewhat in awe of their opponents.

In this picture Arthur de Richemont (1) has ridden ahead of his main force, which stayed on the southern side of the battlefield, and, accompanied by his personal retinue and a unit of mounted archers (2), has hurried to confer with his nominal superior, the young Jean de Clermont (3). The latter had previously sent a small unit of artillerymen under the Genoese Louis Giribault, protected by a force of 200 dismounted *francs-archers* (free archers) under Floquet and 50–60 men-at-arms under De Mauny, to bombard the enemy line. However, the French gunners had been driven back, losing their two cannon when 500–600 English archers suddenly counterattacked. Although this retreat had been covered by French men-at-arms under Pierre de Brézé, losses were suffered and the reverse shook the morale of de Clermont's small army. It must also have contributed to de Clermont's decision to place himself under the command of de Richemont, despite the older man's lower ranking in the feudal order. On the other side, the unexpected appearance of a second French army forced Kyriell hurriedly to redeploy his forces. When the French took advantage of the resulting confusion, the English army collapsed.

The men holding the southern flank of the initial English position outside Formigny saw a new army appear to the south and initially thought that they were friendly reinforcements. (Author's photograph)

his advance guard and mounted archers against the English at the bridge across the Val. The bridge was now taken by the Bretons, whose archers, according to Guillaume Gruel, slew six score of their English opponents. Gruel was actually by de Richemont's side throughout the battle and heard his conversations with other commanders.[5] Arthur de Richemont and Coëtivy now rode forward to study a rapidly changing situation. Coëtivy doubted that the English had really abandoned their laboriously constructed field fortifications, but de Richemont disagreed and apparently convinced de Clermont to order a general advance before returning to his own main force on the other side of the Val.

During the course of this advance, Pierre de Brézé got permission to remount his men and either ride south of, or cut his way through, the English redeployment in order to block the English retreat towards Bayeux. It was a bold move, and for a while the cautious de Richemont hesitated, but, perhaps seeing the increasingly disorganized state of the English, he agreed. The results surely exceeded all expectations, for panic now seized the enemy. Kyriell tried to rally his men to defend Formigny, but Brézé turned against him and overran the village. Several hours of horror ensued, during which the local peasantry joined in to slaughter their English oppressors. One group of 500 or so English archers sought refuge in a garden next to the stream. Throwing down their bows they fell on their knees and begged for mercy, but were nevertheless slaughtered. Gough, meanwhile, gathered a substantial number of his mounted troops and fled to Bayeux, while Robert Vere similarly took his surviving men to Caen.

THE FINAL COLLAPSE IN NORMANDY

Chartier and Gilles le Bouvier record how the heralds carried out their traditional but gruesome task of counting and identifying the dead – 3,768 or 3,774 according to the source – while the corpses were buried by local 'good men' and priests. Among the 1,200–1,400 prisoners were a number of senior men, Chartier listing Thomas Kyriell, Henry Norberry, Thomas Druic (or Driuc, Drew or Dring), Thomas Kirkeby, Christofle Aubercon (or Auberchon),

5 Gruel, Guillaume (ed. A. Le Vavasseur), *Chronique d'Arthur de Richemont, Connétable de France, Duc de Bretagne (1393–1458)*, (Paris, 1890) pp. 206–07.

EVENTS

1 Evening of 14 April: the English, under Kyriell and Gough, marching from the Grand-Vey towards Bayeux, make camp next to the village of Formigny.

2 Night of 14–15 April: a small English outpost is perhaps stationed above Trévières to watch for French movements from the south.

3 Night of 14–15 April: a small English blocking position, probably astride the main road, is established near the top of a slope leading down to the stone bridge.

4 At dawn, Gough heads for Bayeux, perhaps to ask for Somerset's support for Kyriell's attempt to ambush the French under de Clermont.

5 Morning of 15 April: the English construct field fortifications to block de Clermont's approach.

6 The English also construct a small field fortification east of Formigny.

7 An English unit is reportedly guarding the bridge over the river L'Aure.

LE VIEUX PONT

SURRAIN

LES BARRIÈRES

LE HAMEL

CHÂT

8 Having set out from Carentan early in the morning of 15 April, de Clermont's army arrives from the west; de Clermont sends his vanguard under Prigent de Coëtivy, preceded by scouts under Odet d'Aidie, to reconnoitre the English positions.

9 Learning of de Clermont's approach late in the morning, Kyriell arrays his army, with his own troops in front of Formigny and probably across the main road; he sends Gough's mounted troops to the left and closer to the bridge.

10 Gough returns in the early afternoon and retakes command of his troops.

11 Having set out from Saint-Lô early in the morning of 15 April, de Richemont marches towards Trévières, preceded by scouts under the Bastard de La Trémoille and the vanguard under Marshal de Lohéac, Jacques de Luxembourg and Jean II de Brosse; the main body is headed by mounted archers under Gilles de Saint-Simon, Jean and Philippe de Malestroit.

12 Around 3.00pm, de Clermont's main force deploys west of the bridge, then advances until it is about 600m from the English line.

13 de Clermont sends two light guns forward under Louis Giribault, defended by Floquet with 200 dismounted archers and De Mauny with 50–60 lances; the guns bombard the English line.

14 de Clermont sends local peasants to look for de Richemont.

15 Mid-afternoon, de Richemont pauses at Trévières.

16 Gough sends 500–600 archers across the bridge to drive off the French gunners; they capture the guns and pull them back towards the English line.

17 De Richemont crosses the river L'Aure at the Pont de la Barre; a peasant reportedly urges him to hurry because things are going badly for de Clermont.

XXXX

KYRIELL

FORMIGNY

18 French artillerymen, archers and men-at-arms fall back towards de Clermont's main position when attacked by a larger English force; cavalry under Pierre de Brézé probably cover their retreat.

19 Mid-afternoon: de Richemont's troops reach the plateau; de Richemont goes to a windmill to observe the battlefield.

20 When the English see de Richemont's banners to the south they initially mistake them for English reinforcements.

21 When the newcomers are recognized as enemy forces, Kyriell orders a complete redeployment, but the withdrawal of the left under Gough is disrupted by French attacks.

22 De Richemont, with his mounted archers and perhaps his vanguard, discusses the situation with de Clermont; he then sends the vanguard and archers against English archers at the bridge who are guarding the captured guns.

23 Late afternoon: dismounted men-at-arms under Pierre de Brézé retake the guns as the English attempt to redeploy.

24 Late afternoon: de Richemont and Prigent de Coëtivy reconnoitre the English dispositions; de Richemont then probably returns to retake command of his own main force.

25 At the end of the afternoon de Brézé gets de Richemont's permission to remount his men and take the field fortification east of Formigny to block the enemy's retreat.

26 Gough flees to Bayeux with most of the English cavalry; de Vere similarly escapes to Caen.

27 de Richemont advances north-eastwards across the main road to Formigny, crushing the disorganized English.

28 At the end of the afternoon Kyriell attempts to organize a defence of the village, but this is attacked from the west, east and perhaps also south.

29 de Clermont's main force advances, crushing the English attempting to redeploy in defence of Formigny.

30 About 500 English archers are forced into the gardens and orchards of Formigny, where they attempt to surrender but are slaughtered; Kyriell and several commanders are captured, along with large numbers of their men.

THE BATTLE OF FORMIGNY, 15 APRIL 1450
The French turn the English flank and cut their escape route

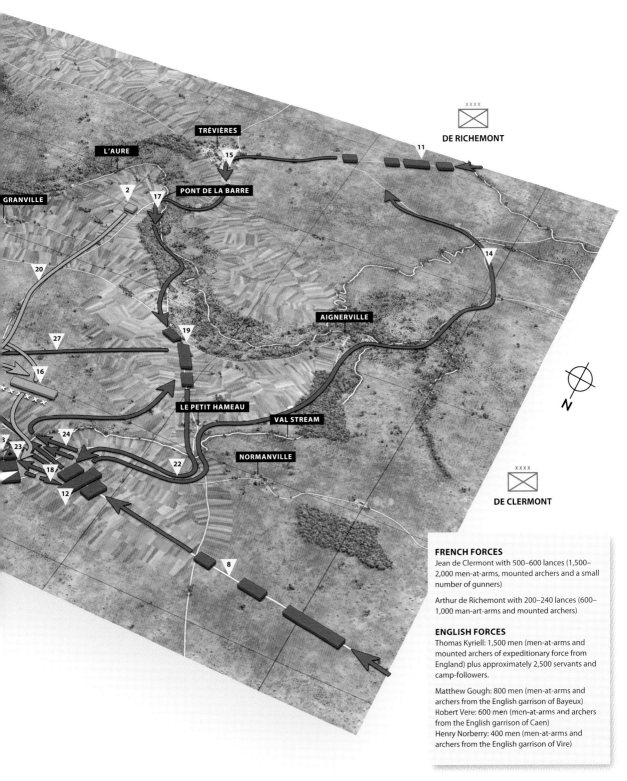

FRENCH FORCES
Jean de Clermont with 500–600 lances (1,500–2,000 men-at-arms, mounted archers and a small number of gunners)

Arthur de Richemont with 200–240 lances (600–1,000 man-art-arms and mounted archers)

ENGLISH FORCES
Thomas Kyriell: 1,500 men (men-at-arms and mounted archers of expeditionary force from England) plus approximately 2,500 servants and camp-followers.

Matthew Gough: 800 men (men-at-arms and archers from the English garrison of Bayeux)
Robert Vere: 600 men (men-at-arms and archers from the English garrison of Caen)
Henry Norberry: 400 men (men-at-arms and archers from the English garrison of Vire)

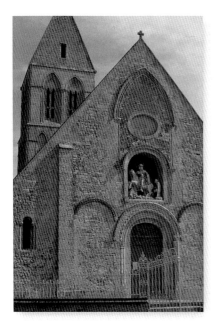

Jean Arpel, Hélix Alengour, Janequin Basceler (or Basquier or Pasquier), Godebert Cailleville (or Caneville) and 'many other English captains and gentlemen who wore coats of arms'. That final comment is perhaps significant as it was only those who were identified as knights who were worth mentioning, and all too often the only ones worth taking prisoner. English sources add the names of William Herbert and Elis Longworth. On the other side, French losses were put at only eight men, which is clearly impossible.

The following day, while the dead were buried, the French army returned to Saint-Lô with its prisoners, remaining there for three days to rest and tend to the wounded. De Clermont and de Richemont also requested orders from Charles VII, asking whether they should now attack Bayeux or Vire. Charles told them to attack Vire, and so this outpost was placed under siege, its demoralized garrison commander surrendering within six days. Now the English held only about half a dozen castles and towns. Charles VII sent the Count of Dunois to besiege Bayeux while Duke François I of Brittany took the plunge and besieged Avranches, where he was joined by Arthur de Richemont. Once Avranches had fallen, de Richemont rejoined Charles VII outside Bayeux but left some troops under his lieutenant, Jacques de Luxembourg, to take over the rest of the Cotentin Peninsula. Bayeux surrendered on 16 May and the French lent horses and carts to those leaving the town. According to the Berry Herald: 'Some carried the smallest of the children in their arms, the next on their poor backs, and the biggest ones they led by the hand.'

Everyone knew that the fate of Caen would settle the outcome of the struggle for Normandy, and in many ways the siege that began on 5 June was even more important that the battle of Formigny. Nevertheless, without direct help from England and barring anything catastrophic happening on the French side, the end was probably inevitable. Four columns marched against Caen under the overall command of René, the nominal King of Sicily, whom Charles VII had put in charge of siege operations, with other princes of the royal blood as his lieutenants. The Abbey of the Holy Trinity and the Praemonenstrian Monastery of Ardenne outside one of the gates of

Caen were chosen as their headquarters, while Dunois established himself in Vaucelles on the road to Paris and de Richemont took up position in the Abbey of Saint-Etienne.

There was, however, no direct assault. Instead, three weeks of relentless bombardment directed by Jean Bureau convinced Edmund Beaufort to request negotiations, resulting in an English surrender on 25 June. Somerset was offered a free passage to England but, anticipating the hostile reception that would await him there, he had himself escorted to Calais instead. A few days later, on 6 July, Charles VII made his ceremonial entry into Caen. His army began its siege of Falaise on the same day. Here the English agreed to capitulate only if the French agreed to release Talbot, which they did. The garrison was then allowed to leave in peace.

After Domfront surrendered on 2 August the only remaining English enclave in Normandy was Cherbourg and the northern part of the Cotentin Peninsula. Even here Bricquebec and Valognes opened their gates to Jacques de Luxembourg, though Saint-Sauveur-le-Vicomte put up a brief resistance in June, leaving just the port of Cherbourg. Here Jean Bureau deserved the final triumph, being in command of the artillery and even devising a system whereby his heavy cannon could be used on the beach despite the coming and going of the tide. Inside Cherbourg the English garrison under Thomas Gower resisted stoutly, causing significant casualties to the besiegers, including Admiral Prigent de Coëtivy. The English also tried to bribe members of Charles VII's Scottish bodyguard, but this failed. Negotiations began, and on 22 August the capitulation of Cherbourg finally brought the Normandy campaign to a close.

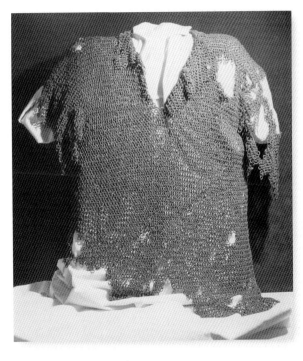

The final phase of the French reconquest of Normandy 1449–50

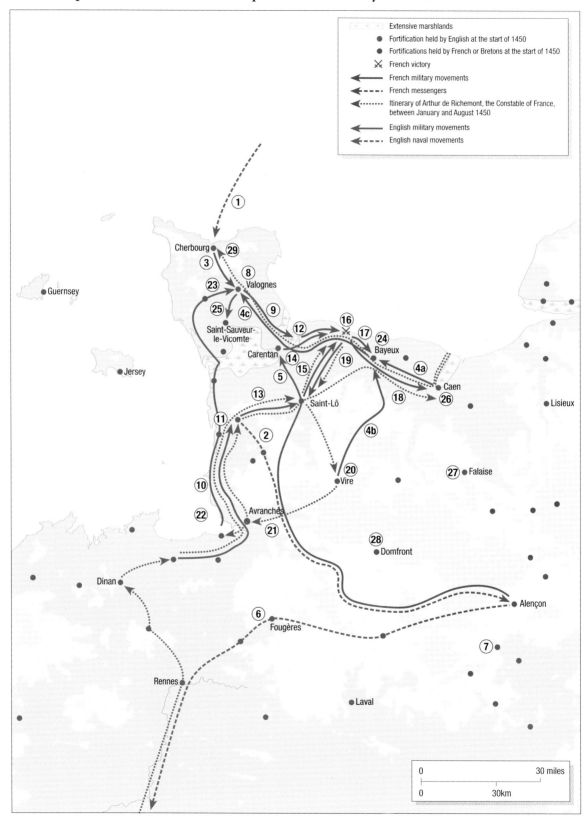

Legend:
- Extensive marshlands
- ● Fortification held by English at the start of 1450
- ● Fortifications held by French or Bretons at the start of 1450
- ✕ French victory
- ← French military movements
- ◄--- French messengers
- ◄····· Itinerary of Arthur de Richemont, the Constable of France, between January and August 1450
- ← English military movements
- ◄--- English naval movements

Guernsey

Cherbourg ③ ㉙
③
㉓ ⑧ Valognes
㉕ ④c ⑨
Saint-Sauveur-le-Vicomte ⑫ ⑯ ⑰ ㉔ Bayeux
Carentan ⑭ ⑲ ④a
⑮ ⑤ ⑱ ㉖ Caen
Jersey ⑬ Saint-Lô
⑪ ④b Lisieux
② ⑳ Vire ㉗ ● Falaise
⑩ Avranches
㉒ ㉑ ㉘ ● Domfront
Dinan ⑥ Fougères Alençon
⑦
Rennes Laval

0   30 miles
0   30km

The carvings on the façade of the 15th-century Hôtel de Ville in Leuven include this representation of the Duke of Burgundy defeating foes on foot, just as French cavalry rode down disorganized English infantry at the battle of Formigny. (Author's photograph)

News of the defeat at Formigny had horrified people in England, and Sir John Fastolf had tried to raise a new army of 3,000 men, but events moved too fast for the situation to be saved. In July a large number of arrows were taken from the Tower of London and sent, with a contingent of fletchers and other skilled workmen, to the remaining English outposts in Normandy. Meanwhile, for most people the shock quickly passed and England got back to 'business as usual'. On 29 June the Duke of Suffolk's ally, Bishop William Ayscough of Salisbury, was murdered in Wiltshire, and on 4 July Lord Say, the Royal Treasurer of England, was killed, his tomb in Greyfriars Church in London being defaced by soldiers who had been 'driven from Normandy' and who now reversed Lord Say's coat of arms as a sign that they regarded him as a traitor.

1 English army under Thomas Kyriell lands at Cherbourg, 15 March 1450.

2 Guillaume de Couvran, the French Captain of Coutances, informs Charles VII of the English landing, 16 March 1450.

3 English attack Valognes, late March 1450.

4a–c Duke of Somerset sends reinforcements from the garrisons of Caen (4a), Vire (4b) and Bayeux (4c) to strengthen the English army, probably arriving after the fall of Valognes, late March 1450.

5 Charles VII sends de Clermont to support Valognes, but is too late; de Clermont establishes himself at Carentan, late March 1450.

6 Jean de Clermont urges de Richemont to march in his support, late March 1450.

7 French seize isolated English outpost of Fresnay-sur-Sarthe, 22 March 1450.

8 Valognes falls to English, 10 April 1450.

9 English resume their march, 12 April 1450.

10 De Richemont's army reaches Granville, 12 April 1450.

11 De Richemont's army reaches Coutances, where a messenger from de Clermont states that the English are apparently marching towards Saint-Lô, 13 April 1450.

12 English cross the Grand-Vey estuary despite local resistance and make camp at Formigny, 14 April 1450.

13 De Richemont takes his army to Saint-Lô, 14 April 1450.

14 De Clermont pursues the English to Formigny, 15 April 1450.

15 De Richemont's army marches via Trévières to Formigny, 15 April 1450.

16 French defeat English at battle of Formigny, 15 April 1450.

17 Matthew Gough escapes to Bayeux, 15 April 1450.

18 Robert de Vere escapes to Caen, 15 April 1450.

19 Combined French armies move to Saint-Lô, 16 April 1450.

20 French take Vire, around 23 April 1450.

21 French take Avranches, 12 May 1450.

22 Bretons under Jacques de Luxembourg take English-held island of Tombelaine, May 1450.

23 Jacques de Luxembourg takes Bricquebec and Valognes, May 1450.

24 French take Bayeux, 16 May 1450.

25 Jacques de Luxembourg takes Saint-Saveur-le-Vicomte, June 1450.

26 French besiege and take Caen, 5–25 June 1450; Charles VII makes a ceremonial entry into Caen, 6 July 1450.

27 French besiege and take Falaise, 6–21 July 1450.

28 French besiege and take Domfront, 23 July to 2 August 1450.

29 French besiege and take Cherbourg, 6 July to 12 August 1450.

THE FALL OF GASCONY

For geographical, logistical and political reasons, it was more difficult for Charles VII to conquer the English-ruled regions of south-western France. Pro-English sentiment was particularly strong in Gascony and Bordeaux, though this was counterbalanced by a new alliance between Charles VII and Count of Foix, who was militarily stronger than the size of his territory might suggest.

French forces had already taken Cognac and Saint-Mégrin in May 1449, followed by Mauléon in September. The Count of Foix had also taken the castle of Guiche, rapidly followed by 15 other castles in the area. Nevertheless, it was the French siege of Jonsac in October 1450 that marked the official start of the new campaign, while far to the north the alliance between Brittany and France was cemented when the new Duke Pierre II 'the Simple' rendered homage to Charles VII.

Meanwhile the English raised a force of 300 men-at-arms and 2,700 archers, which was sent to Bordeaux under the command of Richard Woodville Lord Rivers. Nevertheless, these operations in 1450 were mere preliminaries, after which the French invasion the following year was an almost uninterrupted triumphal march, opening with the capitulation of Montguyon on 6 May 1451.

On 12 June 1451 Bordeaux itself capitulated, followed on the 23rd by the great fortress of Fronsac. Just over a month later the French besieged Bayonne, finally occupying it on 21 August. The rapidity and success of this French campaign appalled the English, but the new regime then imposed such heavy taxes to pay for the defence of these newly conquered territories that resentment spread across Gascony, especially in Bordeaux. Charles VII's government also turned upon the wealthiest man in France, the merchant Jacques Coeur, whom they seemingly expected to use as a cash cow for their new campaign. He was immensely rich and had remarkably far-ranging diplomatic as well as mercantile links while also maintaining strong political connections within France. Nevertheless, Coeur was arrested at Taillebourg on 31 July 1451 and languished in jail from August 1451 until May 1453. Charles VII's 'edict of condemnation' against Jacques Coeur for financial peculation and other crimes was dated 29 May 1453. However, a more serious and clearly ludicrous accusation that he had poisoned the King's mistress, Agnes Sorel, was 'unproven'. It can hardly have been a coincidence that while Coeur was in prison his vast financial assets were available to Charles VII just at the time when a chronic shortage of money threatened to undermine the campaign in Gascony.

Meanwhile, English military preparations were hampered by political problems when, in February, supporters of the Duke of York rose in revolt on

the Welsh borders. They persuaded the Duke to return from Ireland, claim his place on the Royal Council and put an end to what was widely seen as 'bad government'. York's broad support meant that he had little difficulty in raising an army. Meanwhile the Lancastrian court party raised a similar force in London and in March there was an armed stand-off between the two at Dartford, where York presented a list of grievances and demands that included the arrest of Edmund Beaufort. King Henry VI at first agreed, but his formidable wife Queen Margaret intervened and York backed down. He then expressed his loyalty to the King, and Edmund Beaufort was left as the dominant figure in the English government.

Despite such turbulence, a substantial English fleet was assembled during the first part of 1452 and Talbot, who returned to the English court at the end of March, was appointed commander of a new expedition. Only a month after the French first retook Bordeaux, indentures had been authorized for Gervase Clifton, Edward Hull and John Talbot to raise an army. Even as late as 6 July, Talbot's retinue was merely described as an 'army for the keeping of the sea, in which journey he must perform great good', and its official purpose remained equally unspecific on the 18th, though in fact the government had already decided to send it to Gascony. Meanwhile, the English feared an assault on England's remaining enclave of Calais, but in fact Charles VII's next campaign was in a completely different direction, against the territories of the Duke of Savoy in what are now the borderlands of France, Switzerland and Italy. For its part the French government similarly feared an English invasion to retake Normandy and consequently diverted some troops from the south-west to the north of France.

It was one thing to prepare an expedition to retake Gascony; it was quite another actually to launch such a long-distance invasion, but then the English had a huge slice of luck. Many of the leading citizens of Bordeaux already deeply resented the French authorities that now ruled their city, undermining their traditional autonomy and demanding such high taxes. A plot was therefore hatched to bring back their previous rulers. Even after receiving an invitation to return to Bordeaux, the English government's first orders to

The first phase of the French conquest of Gascony 1450–52

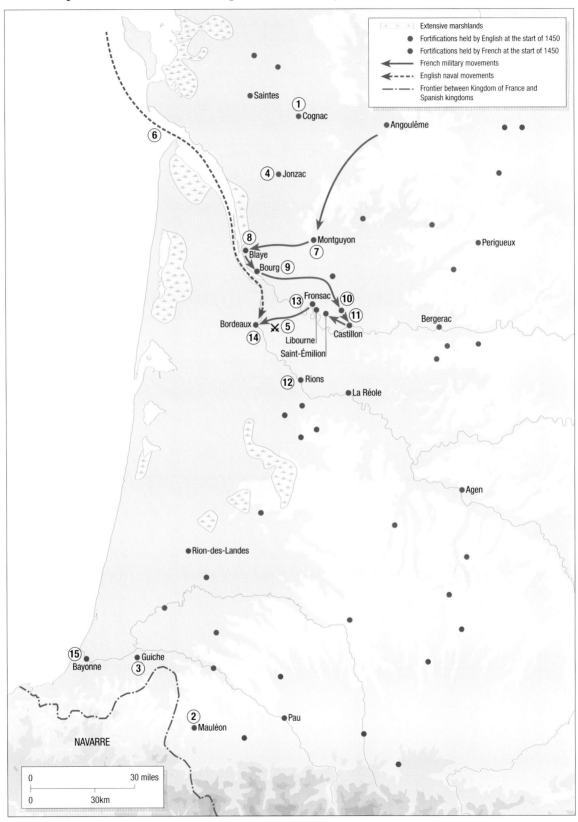

Legend:
- Extensive marshlands
- Fortifications held by English at the start of 1450
- Fortifications held by French at the start of 1450
- French military movements
- English naval movements
- Frontier between Kingdom of France and Spanish kingdoms

Saintes
① Cognac
⑥
Angoulême
④ Jonzac
Perigueux
⑧ Blaye / Montguyon ⑦
Bourg ⑨
⑬ Fronsac ⑩
⑪
Bergerac
Bordeaux ⑤ Castillon
⑭ Libourne
Saint-Émilion
⑫ Rions
La Réole
Agen
Rion-des-Landes
⑮ Bayonne / Guiche
③
② Mauléon
Pau
NAVARRE

0 — 30 miles
0 — 30km

1	French seize Cognac, May 1449.
2	Count of Foix seizes Mauléon, late September 1449.
3	Count of Foix seizes Guiche, February 1450.
4	French invasion of Gascony begins with siege and taking of Jonsac, October 1450.
5	Inconclusive clash between Anglo-Gascon and French forces near Bordeaux, 31 October 1450.
6	English fleet brings reinforcements under Richard Woodville Lord Rivers, autumn 1450.
7	French besiege and take Montguyon, late April to 6 May 1451.
8	French besiege and take Blaye, 15–24 May 1451.
9–11	French besiege and take Bourg, Saint-Émilion and Castillon, 24–29 May 1451.
12	French besiege and take Rions, late May 1451.
13	French besiege and take Fronsac, 2–23 June 1451.
14	Bordeaux capitulates to the French, 23 June 1451; Charles VII makes a ceremonial entry into Bordeaux, 30 June 1451.
15	French besiege and take Bayonne, 31 June to 21 August 1451.

Talbot were to secure the sea lanes now that the entire French coast was in French hands. Talbot would be helped in this task by his fellow commanders: Edward Hull, the ousted English Constable of Bordeaux, who was currently retained for service in Jersey, the largest of the English-held Channel Islands, and Gervase Clifton, who was serving as the treasurer of English-ruled Calais.

The English retaking of Bordeaux and much of the territory around it, though short-lived, was almost as dramatic as the French reconquest that had preceded it. Although the English had wanted to raise an army of around 5,000 men, only 3,000 appear to have set out with Talbot in September 1452. Favourable winds enabled the fleet to reach its destination easily and quickly, disembarking close to Soulac on the Atlantic coast on the northern tip of the Médoc peninsula on 17 October. A nearby creek is still known as 'Englishman's Cove'. According to local traditions the people of this area rose in support of Talbot, several skirmishes were fought and some castles were taken before the invaders reached Bordeaux. There are also indications that the several Gascon lords offered their support to Talbot before he even reached the city.

A strong French garrison of Bordeaux was commanded by Seneschal Alain de Coëtivy, brother of Admiral Prigent de Coëtivy who had been killed in the recent siege of Cherbourg. He was determined to fight but was instead seized in his bed by local people under Louis de Brutails. Coëtivy's 70 soldiers,

LEFT
One of the most detailed carvings of a fully armed mid-15th-century French ship, representing one of the fleet that made Jacques Coeur the richest man in France. (*In situ* Hôtel Jacques Coeur, Bourges)

RIGHT
A mid-15th-century northern-French woodcarving of a type of cargo ship known as a 'barge'. (Musée des Antiquités, Rouen; Yohann Deslandes photograph)

Once the Duchy of Britanny had firmly committed itself to the French cause, French warships could use strongly fortified ports such as Concarneau. (Author's photograph)

who were billeted in local houses, were seized by their hosts the same night in what must have been a carefully coordinated coup, which, according to Thomas Basin, was planned by a middle-class bourgeois named Arnaud Bec. Alain de Coëtivy and his subordinate, Jean de Messignac, were then shipped off to England where Alain remained until the end of 1454.

Once the gates of Bordeaux were opened, the English army entered on 23 October, led by John Talbot wearing the long magenta-coloured coat that had been given to him by Charles VII when Talbot was taken hostage after the surrender of Caen. The people, meanwhile, hailed him as 'Roi Talbot'. Several other places were retaken in November and December 1452, mostly without real resistance. Only the great castle of Fronsac, where Joachim Rouault was based with 600 lances, plus Blaye, Bourg and perhaps some other minor castles, held out. For a while it looked as if Blaye would also fall, until Charles VII sent Boniface de Valpergue and his Italians to secure the place. In most places the French had relied on the fidelity of local garrisons, the majority of which went over to the English as soon as they could.

Surprisingly, perhaps, Talbot began to make the same exorbitant demands upon the people as the French authorities had done before him, seizing 33 ships and gathering taxes that the locals regarded as excessive. In all likelihood Talbot and his French predecessors were simply taking what they believed necessary for the defence of the area. Nor did the newly arrived English troops behave well, pillaging many churches. Amongst the detailed records that survive from this period is one that stated that, as the new English-appointed Constable of Bordeaux, Edward Hull received £437 7s 0d (£410 2s 0d from customs duties on wine exports plus £27 5s 0d from other sources) and paid out in expenditure £1,276 7s 0d, of which £598 was spent on 'war' during a period of nine months in 1452–53. Clearly he was not making a profit from the merchants of Bordeaux and was almost certainly being subsidized from England.

Early in 1453 hostilities were renewed with Talbot's siege of Fronsac. This time the fortress was forced to surrender, though its commander, Joachim Rouault, was allowed to lead his men back to French territory. Meanwhile, in England another army was being prepared to strengthen the English administration in Gascony, and on 7 March 1453 John Talbot's son, John Viscount Lisle, was made 'captain and governor' of this force.

Talbot's success in Bordeaux also had a political impact in England, where public confidence in the government strengthened. The shameful loss of Normandy seems almost to have been forgotten, and the government soon started to take action against those whom it accused of 'dabbling in insurrection in previous months and years'. It would prove to be a bad move. At the same time preparations for Viscount Lisle's new expedition went ahead and in December 1452 ships were 'arrested' or commandeered for royal service at Hull, King's Lynn and Dover. They were first taken to Fowey in Cornwall and then to Plymouth where the fleet was ordered to assemble by 19 February 1453. Despite revived military confidence in many parts of the country, there was still resistance to these 'arrests', resulting in threats of severe punishment and fines. The need for ships was urgent and continued even after the new army under Viscount Lisle sailed to Bordeaux. Indeed ships were still being 'arrested' at London and Sandwich five days before the catastrophic battle of Castillon.

Money seems to have remained a major problem, with the English government resorting to enforced loans, which were similarly resisted as unjust. In Parliament the House of Commons made it very clear that their willingness to supply money to King Henry VI was limited. However, the enlistment of troops seemingly went ahead more smoothly, with 1,325 men

The skyline of the central part of Bordeaux is still dominated by the twin spires of its Cathedral of Saint-André, built mostly when the city was under English rule. (Author's photograph)

known to have been personally retained by Viscount Lisle. Most were infantry, probably archers. By early March, 4,000 men were under the command of Viscount Lisle and Baron Roger de Camoys, along with huge quantities of provisions for them and for those already in Gascony.

Charles VII learned of the perceived treachery of Bordeaux, the news apparently reaching him around All Saints Day at the start of November 1452. He was, of course, furious, and at first threatened to punish the people severely. Charles also sent reinforcements to those places that the French still held and ordered that any suburbs that made them vulnerable should be burned to the ground. He also set about organizing a major campaign to retake the area – for the second time – the following year.

This resulted in the assembling of contingents of cavalry and infantry in regions neighbouring Gascony, while leaving Normandy to be defended by Dunois, known as the 'Bastard of Orléans'. A Milanese ambassador, reporting back to his home city around this time, regarded Charles VII's military preparations as very serious: 'The king and all his officers are making great provision for this war, and are all so intent on it that they pay heed to few other things.'

The French king recognized the difficulties of campaigning so far from the heartlands of his power, and so, bearing in mind the failure of the first French reconquest, he decided to take personal command. According to the Berry Herald, Charles VII installed himself in Lusignan during Talbot's siege of Fronsac, and although he was unable to save that fortress, he did welcome its gallant defender Joachim Rouault when the latter presented himself at Lusignan early in 1453.

Charles VII's diplomatic efforts achieved a breakthrough when Count Gaston IV of Foix agreed to an alliance against the English in Gascony. This led to a useful numerical advantage over the Anglo-Gascon forces in and around Bordeaux. It also meant that English-ruled Gascony could be attacked by four separate armies in a strategy similar to that successfully used in Normandy in 1449. Three columns would head for Bordeaux at approximately

The hamlet of Battlefield and its church of St Mary Magdalene commemorate the battle of Shrewsbury in 1403. The church has a remarkable series of carved gargoyles, mostly in the form of soldiers. (Author's photograph)

A superb illustration of the Story of Roland in a mid-15th-century copy of *Les Grandes Chroniques de France*, made in Burgundian-ruled Belgium or Holland. (Hermitage Library, Ms. Fr. 88, f.154v, St Petersburg)

the same time – one from the south-east, one from east and one from north-east – while Charles VII himself held the 'fourth army' in reserve. The weakness of the strategy was that these forces would be individually outnumbered by Talbot's troops, especially after his son Viscount Lisle arrived.

For the purposes of this account the French army under de Clermont, the King's lieutenant general in Guyenne poised on the southern front, will be called the 'first army'. Having assembled in the Languedoc during April and May, it included *compagnies* commanded by several of the most renowned French soldiers of the day such as the lords of Albret, Orval and Culant, plus Poton de Xaintrailles, the Italian Valpergue and Pierre de Beauvau the Lord of Bessière who commanded forces from Maine. What is here called the 'second army' was under the command of the Count of Foix and included the Viscount of Lautrec, Geoffrey de Saint-Belin the Bailli of Chaumont, Pierre de Louvain, the Bastard of Beaumanoir and other significant captains. It had assembled in Béarn and was ready to cooperate with de Clermont. The 'third army' had assembled in the Angoumois area in April and May, initially under Louis II de Beaumont-Bressuire the Seneschal of Poitou but now under the joint command of Marshal de Jalonges and Marshal de Lohéac, the Admiral of Bueil, Jacques de Chabannes and the Count of Pontièvre. Accompanied by Joachim Rouault, they were poised to operate in the Dordogne Valley. The fourth army formed a strategic reserve under Charles VII, having

assembled in the Lusignan area. Charles VII ensured that the French were also well supplied with siege machines and gunpowder artillery, especially the third army.

The French advance began early in June and with little apparent difficulty retook several small towns and castles. The first and second armies acted together almost from the beginning. After taking control of Saint-Sauveur-le-Vicomte, which may not actually have had an Anglo-Gascon garrison, the two commanders advanced northwards, though separately, across the Bazadais area into the Bordelais region around Bordeaux itself. They then continued into the Médoc area, where de Clermont was met by a herald sent by Talbot, who was carrying a letter dated from 21 June. As the representative of King Henry VI of England, Talbot requested that the counts of Clermont and Foix not damage the countryside, nor harm the 'poor people', because there would be no resistance in that area.

This was recognized as a ploy, but certain courtesies still had to be observed and de Clermont 'requested a meeting' with Talbot in three days' time; thus offering a formal challenge to battle. The armies of de Clermont and Foix were already close to each other, so they agreed to meet at the village of Martignas, which lay between the forests of Candale and Illac. When Talbot heard that his opponents had united, he hesitated and demanded further conditions before agreeing to meet.

Consequently, when the French forces arrived the next day they found no one to talk to, or indeed to fight. Their commanders were, however, told that Talbot had stayed for only a couple of hours to feed his horses before moving on, and that he could not be far away. The French pursued and overtook an ill-fated unit of 500–600 archers, who were said to be exhausted and unable to resist. They may actually have been an ambush party or a rearguard, but whatever their intended role, they were torn to pieces. Meanwhile, Talbot hurried back to Bordeaux while the two frustrated French armies, unable to find enough food when combined as one force, separated and waited in case the English made a sudden sortie from Bordeaux.

The first movements of the third army are not known in detail, but after reaching the Dordogne it, or part of it, seized the castle of Gensac south of the river on 8 July. The troops involved were commanded by Louis II de Beaumont-Bressuire, and included Jean de Bueil and Pierre de Beauvau with 500–600 lances. Meanwhile, Charles VII had left Lusignan on 2 June and went to Saint-Jean-d'Angély, from where he sent Joachim Rouault to besiege Chalais. The attack began on 12 June and more of the royal army arrived two days later, though it is not clear whether Charles VII was present. Chalais fell to assault after a week-long siege, much of the garrison being executed as punishment for so readily opening their gates to the returning English. An Anglo-Gascon relief force under the Lord of Anglade that was hurrying to support Chalais now returned to Bordeaux while Joachim Rouault and his men were sent to join the third army later in June. Thereupon Charles VII either took his army to, or took command of his army at, Angoulême on 17 July 1453.

During this period the third army seems to have advanced slowly and methodically, approaching Castillon from the east in mid-July. The command structure of this force is unclear, with an apparent committee of leaders reflecting its variety of troops. Nevertheless, one man had clearly defined responsibilities; this was Jean Bureau, who was in charge of the siege train and apparently allocated positions in camp, at least when such a camp had field fortifications.

A perhaps detached force under Jean de Bueil crossed the river Dordogne by the Rauzan ford just east of Castillon after the taking of Gensac. It seems unlikely that the main part of this third army with its siege train and numerous cannon would have used such a minor ford. Although the sources do not say as much, it seems probable that they recrossed the Dordogne by the bridge at Sainte-Foy-la-Grande, then made their way along the northern bank to meet Jean de Bueil east of Castillon. Charles VII was of course informed of their progress, and sent orders that Castillon be besieged. This operation began on 13 or 14 July and was said to be under the overall authority of Jacques de Chabannes, but directed by Jean Bureau, Joachim Rouault and the Lord of Boussac. Bureau also had one of Charles VII's most experienced gunners under his command, the Genoese Louis Giribault.

The French army now established outside Castillon was not large but was well equipped, Jean Bureau having around 300 guns at his command, operated by some 700 gunners. The number might have been exaggerated, and the weapons ranged from heavy siege bombards to light hand-held weapons. Estimates of the number of troops vary a great deal, but included 6,000–10,000 men-at-arms, archers and others, plus 700 *manœuvriers* (craftsmen) skilled in the construction of field works under the command of Jean Bureau.

THE BATTLE OF CASTILLON

The town of Castillon was strongly fortified, though in an old-fashioned manner. Beyond its suburbs stood the substantial Benedictine Priory of Saint-Florent on slightly higher ground. A detailed map of the area made in 1762–63 shows the priory in a clearing surrounded on three sides by woods, which was almost certainly also the case in 1453. The small chapel of Notre-Dame de Colles on the northern side of the Rauzan ford also formed a separate part of this priory.

A number of late-medieval hand-held guns still survive, though without their wooden stocks; this 15th-century example was almost certainly made in Flanders. (Castle Museum, Ghent; author's photograph)

EVENTS

1 Substantial Anglo-Gascon garrison defending Castillon as part of a force under Gervase Clifton, which also garrisons Libourne and Saint-Émilion; the English element of Clifton's force consist of 50 men-at-arms and 350 archers, according to payment records before the battle of Castillon. Note that Gervase Clifton does not seem to have been in Castillon at this time.

2 French force, probably troops under Joachim Rouault, probably arrives directly from the taking of Gensac, crossing the Dordogne by the Rauzan ford and initiating the siege of Castillon.

3 On 9 July the garrison in Castillon sends an urgent request for support to the Anglo-Gascon authorities in Bordeaux.

4 It is likely that most of the French army operating in the Dordogne valley, probably under Jacques de Chabanne and including the siege train, recrossed the river at Sainte-Foy-la-Grande after taking Gensac and then approached Castillon along the main road on the northern side of the Dordogne.

5 On 9 July a unit of 700–1,000 archers commanded by Joachim Rouault is sent to the Priory of Saint-Florent.

6 Also on 9 July some 1,000 Breton cavalry and infantry under the sires of Hunaudaye and Montauban are sent to hold Capitourlan and the hills north-east of Castillon.

7 Meanwhile, on 13 or 14 July, on receiving Charles VII's orders to take Castillon, the rest of the army starts constructing a fortified artillery park on the Plain of Colles between the old and new courses of the Lidoire stream, supervised by Jean Bureau.

8 After leaving Bordeaux on 16 July, an Anglo-Gascon army of 6,000–7,000 men under Talbot marches rapidly via Libourne and Saint Émilion, and then follows minor tracks to arrive north of Castillon at dawn on 17 July.

9 Talbot is apparently in contact with the garrison in Castillon, which informs him of the strength of the French garrison in the Priory.

10 Talbot rides ahead of his infantry with men-at-arms and mounted archers through the woods north of Castillon.

11 The Anglo-Gascons attack and take the Priory at dawn on 17 July.

12 French archers defending the Priory are taken by surprise and overwhelmed; their commander Joachim Rouault is not present at the time and the unit may have been under Pierre de Beauvau; from 100 to 120 archers are killed.

13 The surviving French archers retreat to the artillery park, defended by Pierre de Beauvau.

14 Anglo-Gascon men-at-arms, probably under Thomas Evringham, pursue the French archers towards the French artillery park and bring back information about its field-fortifications.

15 About 200 French lances under Jacques de Chabannes hurry to support the retreating archers, accompanied by Joachim Rouault; in the resulting fight Rouault is knocked from his horse and Chabannes is almost captured but the archers reach safety within the fortified artillery park.

16 The Anglo-Gascons find supplies of food and wine in the Priory, so Talbot allows them to rest while he prepares to take mass.

17 The French send varlets and grooms with most of the horses out of the fortified area in order to clear space for a more effective resistance; the horse herds kick up a great deal of dust.

18 Observers in or from Castillon see dust rising from the artillery park and assume that it is caused by a hurried French retreat; Talbot is urged to act immediately; Thomas Evringham advises caution but Talbot decides to attack the enemy as quickly as possible.

19 Talbot leads his mounted troops across the Rieuvert and Lidoire streams and then takes a track along the northern bank of the Dordogne to the Plain of Colles in order to attack the supposedly weaker southern side of the French artillery park; Anglo-Gascon infantry follow at a slower pace, preceded by a mounted guard under Lord Kendall.

20 Realizing that the Anglo-Gascons will attack from the south, the French move their lighter and hand-held guns to face this threat. A vulnerable rear entrance described as a *barrière colisse* is defended by elite troops under Joachim Rouault, René des Peaux and Louis Sorbier.

21 Talbot realizes that the French are not retreating; Thomas Evringham again advises waiting until the infantry arrive but Talbot decides to attack at once, perhaps because the French are still moving their guns; the Anglo-Gascon men-at-arms and mounted archers deploy under eight banners, then Talbot orders Evringham to take Talbot's own banner to the edge of the ditch around the artillery park.

22 Boats from Castillon almost certainly follow the Anglo-Gascon army upstream, but would move more slowly than the infantry.

FIRST PHASE OF THE BATTLE OF CASTILLON, 17 JULY 1453

The English assault the French siege positions outside Castillon

Note: Gridlines are shown at intervals of 500m/1093yds

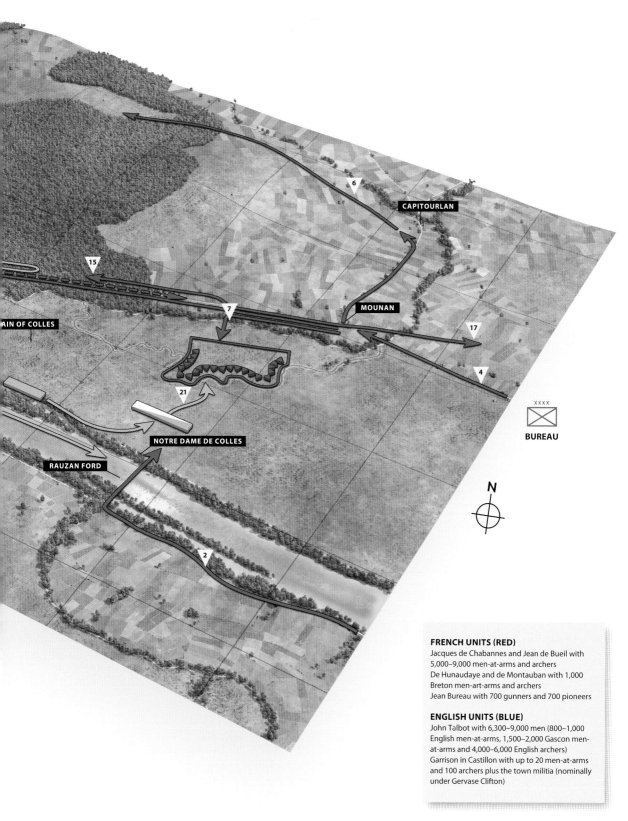

CAPITOURLAN

MOUNAN

15

AIN OF COLLES

7

17

4

21

NOTRE DAME DE COLLES

RAUZAN FORD

2

6

N

XXXX

BUREAU

FRENCH UNITS (RED)
Jacques de Chabannes and Jean de Bueil with
5,000–9,000 men-at-arms and archers
De Hunaudaye and de Montauban with 1,000
Breton men-art-arms and archers
Jean Bureau with 700 gunners and 700 pioneers

ENGLISH UNITS (BLUE)
John Talbot with 6,300–9,000 men (800–1,000
English men-at-arms, 1,500–2,000 Gascon men-
at-arms and 4,000–6,000 English archers)
Garrison in Castillon with up to 20 men-at-arms
and 100 archers plus the town militia (nominally
under Gervase Clifton)

The quayside at Castillon looking up the Dordogne towards the site of the battle. (Author's photograph)

The forests north of Castillon were more extensive in the late-medieval period than they are today. However, they probably did not entirely cover the hills of Horable. The windmills and an open area shown in the 1762–63 map probably existed in the 15th century. These geographical features would play a significant role in the forthcoming battle of Castillon, though the rivers, fords and bridges were even more important. The Dordogne was, and remains, a substantial fast-flowing river, though at this time of the year the water level was low, thus making the ford practical to use.

Of the many smaller streams that flowed into the Dordogne, the Lidoire was small and narrow, but with sides steep enough to form an obstacle to horses if not to men on foot. A factor that has not been sufficiently recognized by military historians is the degree to which the course of the Lidoire changed over the years as it flowed across a narrow strip of flat land on the northern side of the Dordogne. In the 15th century, for example, the Lidoire and a smaller stream called the Rieuvert flowed into the Dordogne at virtually the same point. At a later date this outflow shifted upstream, as shown in sketch-maps made in 1703.

Although the location of the outflow of the Lidoire and Rieuvert would have had minimal significance for the battle of Castillon, the tendency of the Lidoire to shift its bed certainly did. Indeed, a closer inspection of the evidence and of the ground shows that the extraordinarily curvaceous southern side of the French fortified artillery park on the flat land known as the Plain of Colles is actually an old bed of the Lidoire. The only real question is whether it was an old and dry bed in 1453, or was still the course of the stream. Since the sources seem to agree that the field fortifications built under Jean Bureau's direction were on the southern side of the stream, it would seem that this was indeed an old bed, though not necessarily as dry and shallow as now. Indeed today this curving line is no more than a shallow depression used as a field boundary – hence the incorrect assumption that after the battle French farmers made use of Bureau's defensive ditch as a convenient boundary.[6] This

6 The first scholar to identify this depression as the southern edge of the field fortifications was L. Drouyn in *La Guyenne Militaire* (Paris, 1865), the essentials of his interpretation being followed by A. H. Burne's 'The French Camp at Castillon' in *Royal Engineers Journal* (1948) pp. 290-91, and J. L. Nicholson's 'The French Camp at Castillon' in *Royal Engineers Journal* (1949) pp. 156–58.

interpretation assumes that the current relatively straight course of the Lidoire existed in its present form in 1453. Perhaps it was, in fact, made by Bureau's *manœuvriers* or was deepened and straightened by them.

Given the time and number of workmen involved, the extent of the fortified artillery park suggested by most historians seems unlikely, since it would have been substantially larger than the fortified town of Castillon itself. This nevertheless substantial construction was built about 2km east of the town, suggesting that the French expected that the English would attempt to relieve Castillon. They therefore had no wish to be caught between a relieving army and the garrison. Nor was any attempt made to surround Castillon with siege works. Instead a large force of 700–1,000 archers was sent to hold the presumably defensible Priory of Saint-Florent, north-east of the town.

Guns and gunnery were in a state of transition in the mid-15th century, and statements by modern historians that the French had no 'real field artillery' at Castillon miss the point. What Jean Bureau did have were some siege bombards, which were fixed-position weapons designed to batter walls, not to cut down men. They were not really designed to shift their aim once targeted and would have had little role in defending a fortified artillery park, the primary purpose of which was to protect them. At the other extreme, it seems unlikely that the French had many hand-held guns, which could be used by a single man, as the swivelling matchlock was only just coming into use, if it had indeed yet been invented. Similarly there is no evidence that European handgunners carried the small powder horns that made them autonomous fighting units. Instead, most hand-held guns would still have needed two men, one to aim and one to fire. The majority of Bureau's guns were almost certainly quite heavy, relatively long-barrelled but also relatively small-bore and easily aimed. These culverins were anti-personnel weapons, useful in sieges and in the defence of field fortifications if not yet in open battle, though there were apparently also multi-barrelled, smaller-bore ribaudequins.

In addition to the main camp and the garrison in the priory, around 1,000 Breton men-at-arms and archers were sent to hold the village of Capitourlan

The course of the Lidoire has changed since the 15th century, but even in 1453 there was a bridge, so this stream would not have been an obstacle. (Author's photograph)

ANGLO-GASCON VANGUARD SURPRISES THE FRENCH GARRISON OF ARCHERS IN THE PRIORY OF SAINT-FLORENT, DAWN, 17 JULY 1453 (pp. 56–57)

The Anglo-Gascon attack on the Priory of Saint-Florent **(1)** just north-east of Castillon, shortly after dawn on 17 July 1453, caught the French garrison of *francs-archers* by surprise. As a result, Talbot's vanguard of fully armoured men-at-arms and archers **(2)** seized the complex with little difficulty and few casualties. The French defenders **(3)** suffered heavily and had to flee to the fortified artillery park, which formed the main French position east of the town of Castillon. Lord Talbot is unlikely to have led the attack in person. Instead his standard-bearer, Sir Thomas Evringham **(4)**, who apparently took part in the pursuit of the fleeing garrison, may have played a leading role in the assault. Information is similarly sparse on the French side. The *francs-archers* in the priory were commanded by Joachim Rouault and Pierre de Beauvau, but Rouault is known to have been in the artillery park at the time, so in this reconstruction Beauvau **(5)** is given credit for covering the garrison's retreat. He certainly defended the fugitives as they approached the field fortification a kilometre or so away, by which time Joachim Rouault had also mounted up and joined the fight.

and the Horable hills north of the artillery park. They were part of a force sent by the Duke of Brittany, though those sent into the hills were commanded by the lords of Hunaudaye and Montauban. To describe these Bretons as a rearguard is misleading. They would, however, guard against any enemy approach from the north and also serve as a reserve. Subsequent events show that the fortified enclosure on the Plain of Colles was too small to house the entire army and their horses. These dispositions nevertheless meant that the archers in the priory were about a kilometre and a half from the main force, as were the Bretons in the hills.

The main French position was sometimes called a fortified camp, though it seems to have been more of a fortified artillery park. Original sources provide little information, although Martial d'Auvergne in his *Les Vigiles de Charles VII* recorded that Jean Bureau's 700 pioneers (others give the number as 800) laboured from 13–16 July, day and night, making defensive fosses (ditches) 'by compass', which suggests a carefully planned field fortification. These were also 'on three sides', which suggests that the fourth side was adequately protected by something else – presumably the Lidoire stream. The chroniclers state that Jean Bureau's brother Gaspard was also present. These ditches were backed by a palisaded rampart or earthen wall topped by timber defences, which were a standard feature of 15th-century field fortifications.

The English strategy has been widely criticized, largely because it failed. In fact, Talbot's military decisions were fully in accordance with the practices of his time. They offered a good chance of success and were an extension of the English commander's decision to remain in Bordeaux until an enemy army came close enough to be defeated before another could arrive to help it. Nevertheless it is possible that Talbot moved before he really wanted to, the people of Castillon having sent an urgent letter asking the Anglo-Gascon army to raise the French siege. Talbot apparently wanted the enemy to come closer, so that he could pounce more effectively. He would also have been watching the significantly closer armies of de Clermont and Foix. Nevertheless, growing dissatisfaction with Talbot's harsh rule and a clamour that Castillon must be saved threatened to undermine his military prestige.

LEFT
The fortified artillery park constructed by the French lay a few hundred metres south of the foothills, behind the first line of trees seen here. (Author's photograph)

RIGHT
The Château du Roi in Saint-Émilion is dominated by its tall 12th-century keep; the outer defences are late-medieval. (Author's photograph)

Because the English strategy depended upon the complete destruction rather than merely the defeat of the closest enemy force, Talbot had to achieve complete surprise. It is therefore unlikely that the march to Castillon was done without adequate planning. In the event, the Anglo-Gascon army was paraded in the early hours of 16 July. Talbot then marched out of Bordeaux with his men-at-arms and mounted archers, supposedly at 7.00am. Of these troops, 800–1,000 were English men-at-arms and mounted archers, plus perhaps 2,000 Gascon troops under their own lords and 4,000–6,000 English infantry. The size of the French force is highly debatable, and one French chronicler reduced the total number to 5,000–6,000, while the respected French military historian Ferdinand Lot thought that it might have been as great as 8,000 men, with 6,000 in the camp, 1,000 in the priory and 1,000 in the hills.

Although Talbot's force included substantial numbers of foot soldiers, there is no evidence that they lagged behind during the march to Libourne – high summer or otherwise. This strongly fortified town was reached around sunset, but Talbot decided that his men could have only a brief rest before resuming their march, reportedly setting out again at midnight. Whether Talbot now used 'unfrequented tracks through the forest' is unclear, though the English-held town of Saint-Émilion was apparently bypassed, presumably to avoid the risk that news of the English approach would reach the enemy.

After moving past Saint-Émilion the Anglo-Gascons clearly did take to the forests, winding their way through the hills north of the Dordogne. The mounted troops either pressed ahead deliberately, which seems likely, or simply outpaced their infantry. According to Aeneas Piccolomini, the future Pope Pius II, Talbot's mounted vanguard numbered only 500 men-at-arms and 800 mounted archers. Presumably relying on local guides, they assembled in the woods above the Priory of Saint-Florent without the French becoming aware of their presence. It was now approaching dawn on 17 July 1453.

Talbot seemed confident, as were his men, who marched under the banner of a soldier who inspired terror in his foes. What they do not seem to have realized was the fact that French morale and determination was virtually as high as their own. Shortly after the sun rose, the Anglo-Gascon vanguard

60

emerged from the forest and attacked the priory, taking the French archers by surprise. Any patrols that this garrison had out would probably have been watching the roads, not the forests. One of their commanders, Joachim Rouault, was in the fortified artillery park at the time and after a brief-but-bloody struggle the outnumbered defenders fled towards the field fortifications, pursued by Anglo-Gascon men-at-arms.

According to French sources, 100–120 archers were killed at the priory or as they fled along the road. Chartier recorded the difficulty of this retreat along the flank of the hill, fighting hand-to-hand all the way before the survivors crossed the Lidoire 'by a ford or temporary bridge' into the field fortifications. Other French troops who were outside the field fortifications also retreated inside, except for the Bretons in the hills. Meanwhile, the Anglo-Gascon pursuers were met and forced back by 200 French lances of cavalry under Jacques de Chabannes, Rouault and Beauvau, who emerged from the camp to cover the retreating archers. It was only a skirmish, but Rouault was knocked from his horse and Chabannes was for a time surrounded by the enemy before being saved by his men. The pursuers pulled back, but they almost certainly got close enough to the French artillery camp to bring back useful information.

Meanwhile, Talbot and most of his men had found plentiful stores of food and wine in the captured priory. The Anglo-Gascon infantry would now have been coming up and they, like the mounted troops, were told to refresh themselves. Talbot also made contact with the garrison in Castillon, if he had not already done so before attacking the priory. Sir Thomas Evringham may have been amongst those who pursued the French archers or he may have been sent out on reconnaissance after they returned. He certainly brought back a report that gave Talbot pause for thought. Should the Anglo-Gascons follow up their advantage or should the tired troops rest?

Talbot decided not to attack, and he even prepared to take Mass, but then messengers rushed up from Castillon, declaring that there was a cloud of dust over the French camp caused by the French hurriedly retreating. Swearing to his chaplain that he would not hear Mass until he had defeated the French, Talbot gave orders for an immediate attack. Talbot's standard bearer – perhaps Sir Thomas Evringham – is said to have warned that this was a misleading report, but the old commander pushed him aside, supposedly thrusting the flat of his sword against the man's face. If this story is true and if the standard bearer was indeed Evringham, then his subsequent extravagant courage and consequent death would be easily understood. Honour was a sacred but fragile thing on a 15th-century battlefield.

The dust had in fact been completely misinterpreted. It was not caused by the French retreating, but by their sending most of their horses under the care of grooms and servants out of the fortified artillery park. This would provide more room to manoeuvre and perhaps to move their guns. Rather than retreating, the French were preparing to fight without a realistic possibility of flight if things went badly.

Seemingly small details can be significant under such circumstances. One of these was Talbot's clothing at the battle of Castillon. He was reportedly wearing a red velvet surcoat and a purple velvet cap, but no armour because of his previous promise to Charles VII not to 'wear arms' against the French king. Talbot was also on a small but distinctive white riding horse, rather than a *destrier* (a war horse). Because of his age, and perhaps to ensure that his men could see him, Talbot would remain in the saddle after later ordering his soldiers to dismount.

For now, however, Talbot urged his men to hurry, promising them loot in the enemy camp. He led his mounted troops along a path on the northern bank of the Dordogne, crossing the Rieuvert and Lidoire by a wooden bridge, but leaving his infantry to follow as best they could. Yet this was not a disorganized rush and it is likely that the Anglo-Gascons were in a proper array, with a vanguard under Talbot followed by other mounted troops commanded by Lord Kendall to protect the slower-moving infantry. A manuscript called *La Destrousse de Talbot*, which was written before 1461, specifically stated that the English approached in three 'battles' (divisions). Drawing upon the recollections of French participants, French chroniclers recorded how, 'as they arrived the English marched under eight banners, those of England, St George, the Trinity, Lord Talbot, and others skilfully executed'.

According to a letter sent to Charles VII after the battle, part of Talbot's army or its supplies reached the battlefield by boat. These presumably came from Castillon and the little flotilla probably sailed alongside the infantry in Talbot's wake, or it might have been even farther behind. Having marched along the Dordogne, the Anglo-Gascon vanguard now turned to face north, towards the French field fortifications. They would now have seen that the French were not retreating.

For their part, the French would of course have sent scouts to watch the enemy's movements while moving those guns that could be moved (culverins and ribaudequins) onto the earthern ramparts facing the English and similarly rearranging their units. French sources disagree about whether Jean de Bueil or Jacques de Chabannes was in overall command. Indeed, Gilles le Bouvier

was careful to give equal credit to all the senior men and it almost seems as if the army was commanded by a committee. Nevertheless, Jean de Bueil does seem to have been responsible for placing Rouault, René des Peaux and Louis Sorbier in command of the southern entrance. This would be the focal point of the English assault and was described as a *barrière colisse* ('enclosed barrier'). Burne and other military historians were probably correct in locating this where the old course of the Lidoire made a small loop northwards, which would have permitted flanking fire against anyone attempting to break in.

Talbot was undoubtedly taken aback by finding the French standing firm and well prepared. According to the French chronicler Thomas Basin, Sir Thomas Evringham realized the danger of the situation and advised against assaulting a well-fortified position, suggesting that they wait for the infantry before attacking and that they build their own fortified camp nearby.

A stylized manuscript illustration of an army attacking a camp surrounded by timber fortifications pierced with embrasures for guns. (*Jean Chartier's Chronique du Règne de Charles VII*, Bib. Nat., Ms. Fr. 2691, f.131, Paris)

BRETON CAVALRY STRIKE THE FLANK OF THE ANGLO-GASCON ARRAY AS THE LATTER ATTACK THE FORTIFIED FRENCH ARTILLERY PARK EAST OF CASTILLON, LATE AFTERNOON, 17 JULY 1453 (pp. 64–65)

The battle of Castillon is often described as a victory of 'modern' artillery over 'medieval' weaponry and tactics. Although this is an oversimplification, it contains an element of truth. The cavalry vanguard **(1)** of the Anglo-Gascon army under Talbot did dismount to launch a headlong assault upon a French artillery park, which was ringed by field fortifications and defended by large numbers of guns of assorted calibres **(2)**. These guns caused casualties in the English and Gascon ranks, but Talbot's attack was not frontal, because he apparently hoped to hit the less-well-defended rear of the French position. The precipitous nature of this attack may have been owing to a desire to break in before the French deployed all their guns on this southern side. Once the Anglo-Gascons reached the ditch and palisade they fought hand to hand while trying to pull

down the timber defences **(3)**. For their part the French resisted with close-quarter weapons, bows and crossbows as well as firearms **(4)**.

Even when the Anglo-Gascon infantry joined the struggle, the French defenders clung on, giving time for their Breton reserves to reach the camp. While Breton infantry joined the other defenders inside the artillery park, Breton cavalry swung around the perimeter to strike the Anglo-Gascons in the flank **(5)**. At this point Talbot is said to have been wounded, either in the face by a blade or in the arm by a gunshot. A full-scale French counterattack then forced the enemy back to the river Dordogne, where Anglo-Gascon coordination fell apart; Talbot **(6)** and his son Viscount Lisle were killed and their army fled the field.

Evringham also believed that the French could be starved into submission as the local people were largely favourable to the English and would not supply the enemy with food.[7] Evringham was again overruled, the 15th-century chronicler Basin concluding that, 'Talbot still believed that his own name would cow the French into defeat or flight, and also was concerned that any hesitation on his part would undermine this reputation'.

Modern military historians have been even more scathing about Talbot, but the idea that it was the man's pride that forced him to continue an impetuous assault is probably unfair. Allmand concluded that, 'The action smacked too much of the grandiose, if futile, gesture of the French nobility at Crécy just over a century earlier', and Lot also criticized Talbot for making himself such a conspicuous target. Pollard summed up his own feeling by writing: 'Perhaps in the last resort Talbot's weakness as a commander was not that he was reckless, but that merely, in critical moments, he was wanting in judgement.'

Talbot nevertheless had around 10,000 men behind him, even if they had not yet all reached the battlefield, and he may have wanted to attack before his men had second thoughts, but it is more likely that he saw the French placing their cumbersome guns in new positions to face an attack from this unexpected direction. Talbot now ordered his men-at-arms and mounted archers to form up on foot, he alone remaining on his white horse. He then told Thomas Evringham to 'take the banners to the edge of the enemy fosse', in Thomas Basin's words. Evringham obeyed and, with cries of 'St George!' and 'A Talbot, a Talbot!' the first Anglo-Gascon assault tried to break through the defences. Evringham is said to have reached the top of the parapet, but was then shot down. The range was so close that French defenders recalled seeing up to six men being killed by a single shot.

Enguerrant de Monstrelet wrote with obvious satisfaction how, 'Talbot and his men now marched right up to the barrier, expecting to make an entry into the field; but they found themselves courageously opposed by a body of valiant men, well tried in war, which was surprising after the information

7 Basin, Thomas (ed. and tr. C. Samaran), *Histoire de Charles VII, vol. 2, 1445–1462* (Paris, 1965) pp. 195–201.

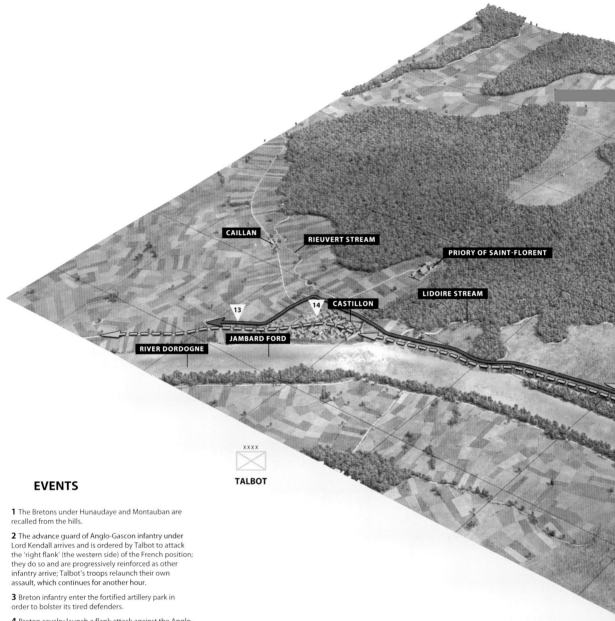

CAILLAN

RIEUVERT STREAM

PRIORY OF SAINT-FLORENT

LIDOIRE STREAM

13

14 **CASTILLON**

JAMBARD FORD

RIVER DORDOGNE

xxxx

TALBOT

EVENTS

1 The Bretons under Hunaudaye and Montauban are recalled from the hills.

2 The advance guard of Anglo-Gascon infantry under Lord Kendall arrives and is ordered by Talbot to attack the 'right flank' (the western side) of the French position; they do so and are progressively reinforced as other infantry arrive; Talbot's troops relaunch their own assault, which continues for another hour.

3 Breton infantry enter the fortified artillery park in order to bolster its tired defenders.

4 Breton cavalry launch a flank attack against the Anglo-Gascons, almost certainly around the eastern side of the fortifications.

5 Talbot is wounded either in the arm by a gunshot or in the face by a blade as the Anglo-Gascons fall back to face a Breton flanking attack.

6 French defenders of the artillery park counterattack, some having remounted horses that remained within the fortifications; they capture the Sire of Moulins.

7 The Anglo-Gascons retreat towards the bank of the Dordogne, where many start to flee across the Rauzan ford; Talbot attempts to rally his troops but his horse is struck by a bullet and falls, trapping him beneath it; Talbot urges his son Viscount Lisle to escape, but the latter refuses and both men are killed as the Anglo-Gascon retreat becomes a rout.

8 The Bretons pursue the enemy to the river, capturing at least five banners, that of Talbot being seized by Olivier Giffart.

9–12 The Anglo-Gascon army collapses; many are drowned as they flee across the river, some escape in boats that had by then reached the ford, while others flee to Castillon and beyond to Saint-Émilion.

13 French cavalry under the Comte de Pontièvre and others pursue fugitives as far as Saint-Émilion.

14 The French besiege and bombard Castillon, which surrenders on 30 July; Jean de Grailly, the Lord of Montferrant, the Sire of Anglades, the Sire of Rosan and other senior men are captured.

FINAL PHASE OF THE BATTLE OF CASTILLON, 17 JULY 1453
The Breton flanking attack and French counterattack crush Talbot's force

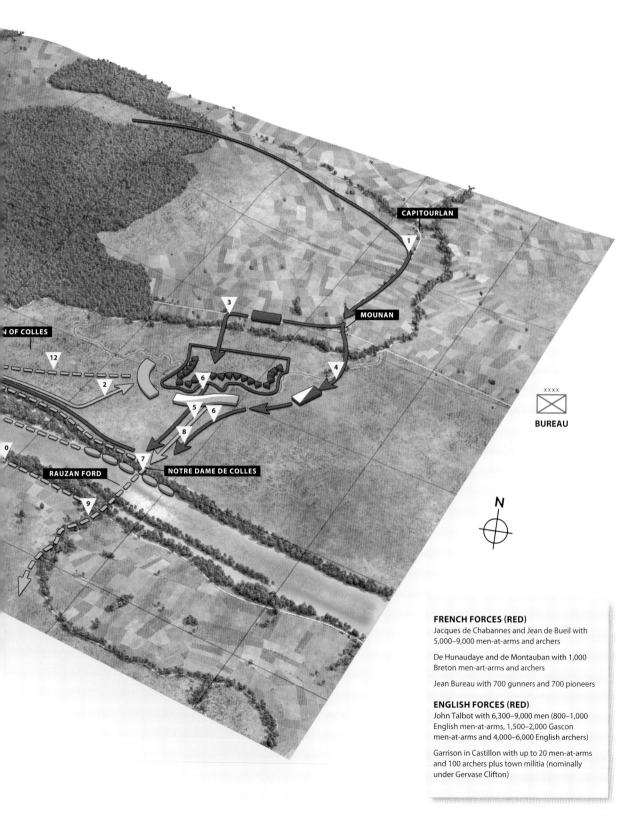

CAPITOURLAN

1

3

MOUNAN

N OF COLLES

12

4

2

6

5 6

8

XXXX

BUREAU

7

RAUZAN FORD

NOTRE DAME DE COLLES

9

N

FRENCH FORCES (RED)
Jacques de Chabannes and Jean de Bueil with
5,000–9,000 men-at-arms and archers

De Hunaudaye and de Montauban with 1,000
Breton men-art-arms and archers

Jean Bureau with 700 gunners and 700 pioneers

ENGLISH FORCES (RED)
John Talbot with 6,300–9,000 men (800–1,000
English men-at-arms, 1,500–2,000 Gascon
men-at-arms and 4,000–6,000 English archers)

Garrison in Castillon with up to 20 men-at-arms
and 100 archers plus town militia (nominally
under Gervase Clifton)

they had received'. Like Chartier, he nevertheless admired the fortitude and courage shown on both sides. Particular credit was given to the senior gunner, Louis Giribault, and his assistants. Elsewhere, an array of other weapons was used in brutal close combat, including axes, guisarmes and spears, and there is also mention of bows and crossbows being used.

Given the short distance between the priory and the battlefield it cannot have been a full hour before the Anglo-Gascon infantry arrived. Yet it was only now that they are said to have appeared. Some have written that this main body crossed the Lidoire on Talbot's left, which might suggest that they marched along the main road rather than along the Dordogne. Whatever precise route these infantry took, they appeared piecemeal under the leadership of Lord Kendall. Talbot ordered him to attack the right flank of the French position, and when Kendall pointed out that he had only the leading elements of the force under his command, Talbot told him to throw in other units as and when they arrived.

The eventual numbers of Anglo-Gascons engaged outnumbered the French, and although the latter were behind field fortifications the French chroniclers admitted that the defenders were tiring. The arrival of Kendall's infantry also seems to have revived the spirits of Talbot's own men. So the struggle continued for a further hour. The Anglo-Gascons were then struck a devastating flanking blow by Breton cavalry that had come down from the hills.

Several questions remain unanswered about this Breton attack. Why did it take so long to appear? Did the French commanders hold off until they could see their foes tiring, or had the Bretons been held back in case the bulk of Talbot's infantry came down the main road to attack from the north? What is known is that Breton men-at-arms and perhaps mounted archers under Montauban and Hunaudaye caught Talbot's men in the flank, almost certainly striking their right having swept around the eastern side of the artillery park. Meanwhile, other Bretons, presumably infantry, hurried into the fortified area through its northern entrance across the Lidoire to replace the exhausted defenders at the southern entrance. The fact that this assault caught Talbot by surprise probably resulted from the amount of smoke and noise caused by the primitive guns.

As Talbot turned to face this attack he appears to have been wounded. According to Thomas Basin he was struck in the arm by a bullet from a serpentine or culverin, though another version has the English commander half blinded by a facial wound. What is certain is that the French, seeing their enemies falter and encouraged by the Breton assault, launched a ferocious counterattack from inside their field fortifications. The oldest account of the battle, in a letter written just two days later by an unknown author to friends in Angoulême, noted that there were still some horses within the fortifications and that some French men-at-arms remounted to take part in this attack.

According to Thomas Basin, the French reached Talbot's son Viscount Lisle and killed him, but others insist that Lisle and Talbot were slain together at the end of the battle. The precise chronology of events in the Anglo-Gascon army is impossible to define as it fell back towards the Dordogne and the ford. Panic was already spreading and cohesion would have been lost as the banners fell. Enguerrant de Monstrelet wrote that these were trampled underfoot, whereas the second-oldest account of the battle, a letter sent by Charles VII to the people of Lyon on 22 July, stated that the banners of St George and the King of England, along with the standards of Talbot and others, were captured. Chartier specified that the Anglo-Gascon banners were taken and reversed by the Bretons, making them invisible to the English and Gascon troops who fought beneath them – a significant matter in a medieval battle. Talbot's own banner was seized by Olivier Giffart and was almost certainly amongst the five taken to Brittany.

Gilles le Bouvier seems to say that the Sire of Moulins – Robert Hungerford Lord Moleyns – was captured immediately outside the *barrière*, which would indicate that some of the Anglo-Gascons were cut off when the rest of their comrades retreated. Talbot now attempted to rally his men, or at least to make a stand so that others could escape across the Rauzan ford, and it was here that he died, probably alongside his son. A family legend claimed that when the aged Talbot was trapped beneath his wounded horse he urged his son, Viscount Lisle, to flee, saying: 'Leave me, the day belongs to the enemy, there is no disgrace in flight, this is your first battle.' Lisle refused to do so, and the leadership of the Talbot family went to his illegitimate half-brother.

Another version recorded by Vallet de Viriville had Talbot wounded by a culverin, but confirmed that he became trapped beneath his fallen horse and was killed by archers. Another variation has the horse rather than Talbot being wounded by the bullet, but the general consensus was that Talbot received no pity because he had shown none. He who had lived by the sword had died by sword and, according to Thomas Basin, 'His companions were also killed without pity'. Elsewhere it was suggested that the old man was not recognized, and so a potentially large ransom was lost.

A singularly brutal account of Talbot's death is found in that anonymous letter dated 19 July 1453. It maintained that Talbot was killed by a French archer who thrust his sword so far up the old warrior's rectum that its point appeared at his throat. The probable truth was only marginally less appalling. While trapped beneath his horse, John Talbot was struck on the head by a French soldier, perhaps an archer, named Michael Perunin, who was wielding an axe. Centuries later, when Talbot's tomb was opened in 1873, the top of his skull was indeed seen to have a large hole in it that had been made by an edged weapon. A mouse had made its nest inside.

When the demoralized Anglo-Gascon army realized that Talbot was dead, it collapsed entirely. One story holds that Talbot's injured horse regained its feet and, by galloping free, spread further panic. Large numbers of men fled the way they had come, 800–1,000 finding refuge within the fortified town of Castillon. Others pressed on to Saint-Émilion and Libourne. Many of those who tried to cross the Dordogne by the Rauzan ford were said to have drowned, though they are likely to have been those already injured. Others succeeded, dispersing across the countryside or heading westwards towards Bordeaux. A lucky few are said to have clambered aboard the boats that had apparently followed the army.

A small number of French cavalry under the Count of Pontièvre, the Bailiff of Touraine and others harried the fugitives as far as Saint-Émilion, but most of the French army was too exhausted to pursue. Castillon was promptly placed under siege while the news of the victory was sent to Charles VII at La Rochefoucauld, reportedly reaching him less than half a day later. He immediately ordered a celebration and the singing of a Te Deum in the castle chapel.

There is wide disagreement about the number of Anglo-Gascons killed. Gilles le Bouvier puts it between 3,000 and 4,000, including those cut down in the subsequent pursuit. Chartier is more conservative, stating that 30 knights were slain as well as 500–600 English soldiers. He does not mention Gascon casualties. Martial d'Auvergne and Vignier agree on the 30 knights, but add 2,000 English and 800 'others', presumably meaning Gascons, while Enguerrant de Monstrelet merely wrote that, 'Some four or five hundred English were buried by the French'. Most men-at-arms, though fully armoured professional soldiers, were not actually of knightly rank.

Only the most senior or famous of the dead were named. According to Gilles le Bouvier and Chartier they included Talbot and his son Viscount Lisle, the knights Edward Hull and Thomas Evringham and the Gascon lord of Puy-Guilhem in the Comminges region. The only senior figure to be captured on the battlefield was Lord Moleyns, though many more would be taken when Castillon fell, including the Gascons Jean de Grailly and the Lords Monferrant, Rauzan and Anglade, amongst others. The Lord of Lesparre did not pause at Castillon but fled directly to Bordeaux, perhaps knowing that the French regarded him as a leader of the 'treason' that had brought the English back to Gascony.

French losses were far less severe, though still significant. In addition to those archers killed when the Anglo-Gascons seized the priory, the fighting in and around the field fortifications had been fierce. Although no senior men had been lost, Jean de Bueil, Jacques de Chabannes and Pierre de Beauvau had all been wounded, de Bueil proudly proclaiming that he had suffered two wounds.

As was normal practice, the dead were buried the day after the battle. There are a number of accounts regarding the identification of Talbot's body. Some merely say that, despite his disfigurement, the English commander was identified by his captured squire on the basis of an old wound. Another version elaborated upon this account, claiming that Talbot's herald returned to the battlefield the following day in the hope of finding his master amongst the captives. This story has the man recognizing Talbot because of a missing tooth, whereupon he fell on his knees and cried out: 'My master, my master, is this you? I pray to God that He may forgive your sins. I have been your *officier d'armes* for 11 years and more. It is time that I must give you up.' Thereupon the herald covered Talbot's body with the old man's coat of arms.[8]

Jean Bureau apparently insisted that John Talbot be buried with full honour in the nearby Chapel of Notre-Dame de Colles. Jacques de Chabannes meanwhile sent Talbot's banner and *gorgerette* (collar of office) to Charles VII. On receiving them, Charles reportedly said, 'God have mercy on a good knight', and then sent letters to the main cities of France ordering that the victory be marked by religious celebrations. It was also said that Talbot's *brigandine* (a light form of textile-covered scale-lined armour) ended up in the Château d'Amboise, and if this is true then the English commander was wearing a light form of armour after all, presumably beneath his magenta-coloured cloak.

Some time later Talbot's body was reinterred at Falaise in Normandy, but even then it had no rest, the brain being removed and sent for burial at Whitchurch in Shropshire, where it was rejoined by the rest of Talbot's body around 1493. This grave was opened yet again in 1860, confirming that, 'the true cause of death was seen to be a blow from a battle-axe on the skull'.

Immediately after the battle, the French turned their attention to the fortified town of Castillon. It took a few days to get Jean Bureau's cannon into position, but a bombardment started on 18 July and, despite resistance from the local Gascon lords, the English garrison surrendered two days later. The actual capitulation was signed in the neighbouring village of Saint-

8 Lodge, E. C., *Gascony under English Rule* (London, 1926) p. 133.

Etienne-de-Lisse. According to Enguerrant de Monstrelet this surrender placed a further 1,500 prisoners in French hands and , 'the chief lords among them were made the personal prisoners of the king'.[9]

After any major battle the victors scoured the battlefield for useful military equipment, but it is rare for this practice to be reflected in the archaeological record. Castillon was an exception, with about 80 swords being recovered from the Dordogne, some way upriver from the town of Castillon, in the 1970s. Having been found in the remains of two wooden casks, they cannot have been simply dropped by fleeing English or Gascons and they are now believed to have been booty placed aboard a ship that then sank.[10] Talbot's own sword was reportedly recovered from the Gironde estuary many years later, then supposedly appearing in an engraved copy of a portrait of Talbot published by André Thevet in his *Vrais portraits des hommes illustres*.[11]

The events around Castillon caused friction within the French army, and on 23 July Charles VII sent two senior men to conduct an investigation. After a deal of toing and froing by royal messengers, Charles VII concluded that his presence was needed at the front to maintain control for the rest of the campaign. A potentially serious problem, given the prickly honour of the late-medieval French aristocracy, concerned who should take ultimate credit for victory at Castillon. Both Jacques de Chabannes and Jean de Bueil claimed this honour, and as a result a fierce quarrel developed between the two men, who had previously been friends. Indeed, this quarrel continued even after

Part of a large panel painting of members of the aristocratic French family of Jouvenal des Ursins, four of the young sons being shown as fully armoured mid-15th-century knights. (Musée Médiévale, Paris; author's photograph)

9 Thompson, P. E. (ed.), *Contemporary Chronicles of the Hundred Years War* (London, 1966) pp. 339–40.
10 Oakeshott, E., 'The Swords of Castillon' in *The Tenth Park Lane Arms Fair* (London, 1993) pp. 7–16.
11 Thevet, A., *Vrais portraits des hommes illustres* (Paris, 1584) folio 282; this in turn was the subject of a study by M. Teulet, a member of the Société des Antiquaires de France, in 1856.

Jacques de Chabannes died not long afterwards, either from wounds suffered at Castillon or more likely from the pestilence that broke out during the final siege of Bordeaux. Jean de Bueil almost got involved in a duel with Chabannes's supporter, La Vaissière, and when the latter also died within a few years his brother Dammartin took over both his military command and his quarrel with de Bueil.

THE END OF ENGLISH GASCONY

These problems within the French army were as nothing compared to those facing the remnants of the English and Gascon forces in and around Bordeaux. Their remaining strongholds now fell one by one, with the town of Saint-Émilion going down almost without a struggle, closely followed by its castle. Not only were the dispirited and now outnumbered defenders of such places facing Jean Bureau's numerous cannon, but the surrounding countryside was being harried by units of men-at-arms, including Valpergue's Italians.

From Saint-Émilion the French army moved against Libourne, which was larger and stronger. There they were joined by Charles VII, who had taken the fourth army to Angoulême on 17 July 1453. From there he set out on the 28th via the Abbey of La Couronne to make his way to Libourne. Accompanying Charles VII were the counts of Maine, Angoulême, Castres, Vendôme, Etampes and Nevers – all princes of the realm. At Libourne this distinctly 'royal' army joined forces with the troops who had won the battle of Castillon and Charles took command of the siege. Faced with such an army headed by a king, and despite their long tradition of loyalty to the English Crown, the inhabitants now handed Libourne and its English garrison over to Charles VII.

The fortified town and port of Libourne overlooked the junction of the rivers Dordogne and Isle. (Author's photograph)

LEFT
This small illumination in the mid-15th-century *Legend of Troy* shows a confrontation between equally balanced armies of cavalry and foot soldiers. (Bib. Roy., Ms. 9240, f.58r, Brussels)

RIGHT
'The Argonauts landing at Colchis', in a 15th-century French manuscript of Greek legends. (Bodleian Lib., Ms. Douce 353, f.31, Oxford)

On 8 August Charles VII and de Clermont appeared before the powerful fortress of Fronsac, which offered no resistance. By now it was clear that the presence of the French King made it easier for places to surrender without loss of face. Charles next entered the Entre-Deux-Mers region and on 13 August established his headquarters in the castle of Montferrant, facing Bordeaux across the river Garonne. Bertrand, the Lord of Montferrant, was one of those Gascons who now transferred his allegiance to the King. One part of Charles VII's army camped a few kilometres to the north at the river-port of Lormont while another part, including specialist troops under Jean Bureau, went to strengthen the Count of Foix's siege of Cadillac.

It would be wrong to think that the English in Bordeaux simply accepted their fate passively. In fact, Roger de Camoys was named Seneschal of Guyenne after Talbot's death at the battle of Castillon. He promptly tried to rush reinforcements to Libourne, Cadillac and Blanquefort. He also sent men to defend a newly constructed *bastille* (outer defence work) at Bordeaux, as well as the existing gates and fortifications. This *bastille* served to protect Bordeaux's riverside harbour and the ships it sheltered. Apart from a shortage of troops, Roger de Camoys' biggest fear was that many Gascon lords would now defect to Charles VII; some did, but not as many as might have been expected. Roger de Camoys was meanwhile supported by Thomas Clifton, the Bastards of Somerset and Salisbury and those Gascon lords who had made their way back to Bordeaux after the disaster outside Castillon, including the lords of Lesparre, Rauzan and Duras.

Financial records for the period 20 October 1452 to 20 October 1453 provide interesting information about English garrisons during the final months of English rule. They were clearly established at Sauveterre, La Marque and Bénauge, though no payment for soldiers was allocated to the last of the outposts after 17 July 1453, perhaps indicating that it was abandoned. In contrast, the garrison of Rions almost doubled in size after the battle of Castillon. At Langon there were again no recorded payments after 10 May 1453, or at Saint-Macaire after 17 July 1453, perhaps again indicating that they were abandoned. However, the number of troops in Bordeaux greatly increased, with the arrival of new contingents during this period.

During the final French siege of Bordeaux a French fleet was assembled at La Rochelle, where the fortifications had recently been greatly strengthened. (Author's photograph)

The garrisons of Libourne and Saint-Émilion were still considered to be a single formation, though the third section of this unit at Castillon was lost following the battle there. The triple garrison had been under Gervase Clifton, who had sailed from England with Talbot, and included 50 men-at-arms and 350 archers, whose wages came to 6,750 Bordeaux francs. As such, it was the biggest garrison until that of Bordeaux was increased. John Courtenay was a captain in Bordeaux with 20 men-at-arms and 200 archers, as was Talbot's son Viscount Lisle with 30 men-at-arms and 300 archers until he was killed at the battle of Castillon. Subsequent payment records show Gervase Clifton with 60 men-at-arms and 400 archers as a captain in Bordeaux from the day of the battle of Castillon, probably until 20 October 1453, though this is not entirely clear.

At Cadillac the last recorded payment to a garrison was on 25 March 1453. From the date of the battle of Castillon until its surrender around 18–20 July, the Cadillac garrison was commanded by a man named Gailardet, though there were also other officers there, with 60 men-at-arms and 300 archers. An unnamed captain held the Bastille des Chartrons at Bordeaux with 30 men-at-arms and 80 archers from the day of the battle of Castillon until perhaps 1 October, while Louis Despoy held the Convent of Clarisses at Bordeaux with just 200 archers, probably until 20 October. During this same period the smaller Bordeaux garrisons were those under Asseguin Gentil with ten men-at-arms and 30 archers at the Archbishop's Palace in Bordeaux, and a captain named Ysalsenat with a mere five men-at-arms and 20 archers at the Mill of Sainte-Croix.[12]

12 Vale, M. G. A., *English Gascony 1399–1453* (Oxford, 1970) pp. 240–41.

These remarkable medieval English bureaucratic records also give the names of the men who held certain posts, highlighting when these positions were lost. For example, Roger de Camoys was appointed as Seneschal of Guyenne by King Henry VI on 4 July 1453 and was still active on the day before Bordeaux capitulated. Henry VI actually appointed a successor, William Bonneville, on 12 September 1453, but this man never took up his position. On the other hand, John Talbot was the last English Lieutenant of Guyenne, no successor being appointed from his death until the final collapse of English authority some months later. The Constable of Bordeaux was Edward Hull, who nominally still held this position during the first period of French reconquest. Like Talbot, he was killed at Castillon and no replacement was selected.

While the English were trying to reassemble something from the wreckage, the other French armies operated elsewhere in Gascony. The counts of Clermont and Foix, for example, were still in the Bas-Médoc area at the time of the battle, ravaging the countryside to deny food supplies to the Anglo-Gascon troops in Bordeaux. On 14 July they attacked Castelnau, where the garrison, commanded by Gascon de l'Isle, did not resist for long. They then besieged nearby Châteauneuf-de-Médoc. De Clermont next led his army towards Bordeaux, hoping to take Blanquefort by surprise. However, this famous old castle with its six towers held by Gailhard de Durfort had closed its gates after news of the battle of Castillon. A sudden assault failed, and a siege was now required.

Meanwhile, the Count of Foix headed south and arrived before the fortifications of Cadillac at the head of some 400 lances and 5,000–6,000 crossbowmen. The Gascon captain, Gaillardet, was in command of Cadillac and he promptly went to Castelnau with an offer of submission. This, however, seems to have been a ruse to gain time and Gaillardet either withdrew his offer or demanded unacceptable conditions. Whatever the case, a full-scale siege again proved necessary. Cadillac was very strong and it continued to defy them even after Chabannes, the Count of Castres, the Marshal de Jalonges and Jean Bureau arrived with 800 lances and powerful artillery. Indeed, the siege dragged on for so long that two substantial bodies of troops were detached to mop up other Anglo-Gascon outposts. One, commanded by Xaintrailles, was sent against Saint-Macaire while the other under the Lord of Albret quickly seized control of Langon and Villandraut.

Thus two major sieges were now under way north and south of Bordeaux, which was itself threatened by the largest French armies, now commanded by Charles VII. According to Chartier there were still 8,000 English (or, more likely, English and Gascon) troops in Bordeaux. They, it seems, were not active in defence but remained passive. Morale must have been low, not least because a number of important Gascon lords continued to transfer their allegiance to Charles VII. One of these was Gaston de L'Isle, who was 'forgiven' by the Count of Foix on 20 July, having handed over Castelnau and some other places six days previously. Meanwhile, the campaign against Bordeaux was more of a blockade than a siege. Charles VII remained close to the front, directing operations throughout September, but in October an epidemic, described as usual as 'plague', broke out in the French ranks. Those who succumbed included Jacques de Chabannes, who was serving as *grand maître* (grand master) of the King's household, and Pierre de Beauvau. A rapid conclusion to the campaign was necessary.

The monumental brass of T. de Saint-Quinton, in the parish church of Harpham in Yorkshire, dates from 1445 or a few years later and shows a fully armoured English man-at-arms in typical armour of the period.

A surviving part of 14th-century urban fortifications near the Church of Saint-Croix in Bordeaux. (Author's photograph)

Some units of the army that had fought at Castillon had meanwhile been sent elsewhere, though there is no evidence that this dispersal was linked to the threat of disease. One such was the unit of archers commanded by Joachim Rouault, who himself disappeared from accounts of the final phase of the campaign. For reasons that remain unknown, his archers were sent to the southern Auvergne, where the bad behaviour of at least one of them left its mark in local legal records. The man in question was billeted in the house of a civilian named Yvonnet Carrachat in the small village of Ytrac, just west of the town of Aurillac, where Joachim Rouault's men had arrived in August 1453. Like some soldiers everywhere, he tended to boast of his recent heroic exploits, as recounted by the French historian P. D. Solon:

> An archer, his two servants, and an unidentified woman and child were quartered in Carrachat's house. Anxious to please, Carrachat greeted his guests with wine upon their arrival, only to hear the archer announce his intention of seducing Carrachat's wife. The archer thereupon rode off to rob the church to pass the time until dinner. Upon his return, the guests dined regally while being entertained with the archer's tales of his prowess. When a fight broke out after dinner, the archer was killed while attempting to eject Carrachat from the house'.[13]

When this unhappy episode was brought to Charles VII's attention, he pardoned the unfortunate house-owner.

13 Solon, P. D., 'Popular Response to Standing Armies in Fifteenth Century France' in *Studies in the Renaissance*, 19 (1972) p. 89.

Meanwhile, the siege of Bordeaux was difficult for a number of reasons. The city was large by medieval standards, having a circumference of 6,000m, and it had three walls with 20 large towers and a number of strongly defended gates. The eastern side was also protected by the broad river Garonne, which, in the 15th century, was at least 600m wide. Bordeaux's port also contained a formidable fleet, and, as a result, the only way to completely invest the city was to assemble an opposing fleet.

While the necessary ships were being assembled, French forces continued to roam the surrounding area to ensure that no supplies reached the besieged. One of the units involved was the Scottish *compagnie* commanded by Pettilot. Charles VII did not take part in such actions, but instead moved to and fro between his headquarters at Montferrant, the river-port of Lormont and Saint-Macaire, while probably also making morale-boosting visits to the siege of Cadillac, where an Italian *compagnie* under Theaulde Valpergue was engaged.

The first French assault on Cadillac took control of the town but not its formidable castle. The English garrison now demanded 6,000 *écus* (an *écu* was a coin of significant value), plus other rewards, as the price of their surrender. Charles VII may have felt such haggling to be beneath his dignity, so he left the matter to commanders on the spot. Eventually an agreement was reached with the soldiers, though perhaps not with their leader. Cadillac capitulated and the garrison was taken prisoner, but their commander, Gaillardet, was executed. The nearby Anglo-Gascon outposts of Bénauges and Rions then surrendered.

This enabled most of the French army to concentrate on the siege of Bordeaux, though de Clermont's force continued to operate in the coastal area of Médoc. With the English cause collapsing on all sides, Gailhard de Durfort the Lord of Duras also negotiated the surrender of Blanquefort with

A 15th-century Flemish tapestry showing a two-man team firing a substantial hand-held gun. (Musée d'Equitation, Château of Saumur; author's photograph)

de Clermont, who then crossed the marshes to Bordeaux. Inside the city, conditions were becoming desperate. The siege eventually lasted ten weeks but the new English leader Roger de Camoys refused to negotiate until it was obvious that no relief would come from England. To ensure that no one fled by sea he had the masts removed from all ships, and then used the hulls as floating batteries to protect Bordeaux's harbour. The population's morale had clearly been shattered by Talbot's defeat and death at Castillon. This, together with worsening privation within the city, led to increasing tensions between the English and the Gascons. The epidemic that had broken out in the French

1 English fleet under Talbot arrives outside the Gironde estuary; its troops disembark near Soulac-sur-Mer, 17 October 1452.

2 The English under Talbot retake Bordeaux, 23 October 1452.

3 Joachim Rouault, the French Constable of Bordeaux, falls back to Fronsac, October 1452.

4 French reinforcements under Boniface de Valpergue rushed to Blaye, October 1452.

5 English retake Blanquefort, November 1452.

6 English retake Libourne, Castillon and Saint-Émilion, November–December 1452.

7 English retake Rions, Cadillac, Saint-Macaire and Langon, November–December 1452.

8 English fleet under John Viscount Lisle arrives at Bordeaux, late March 1453.

9 English under Talbot besiege and take Fronsac, March–April 1453; Talbot returns to Bordeaux.

10 Joachim Rouault joins Charles VII at Lusignan, late April or May 1453.

11 Charles VII assembles an army as a reserve at Lusignan, April–May 1453.

12 Army under Count of Foix assembles in Béarn, April–May 1453.

13 Army initially under Louis de Beaumont-Bressuire assembles in Angoumois area, April–May 1453.

14 Army under Jean de Clermont assembles in Languedoc area, April–May 1453.

15 Official start of French campaign to retake Gascony, Charles VII leads French army to Saint-Jean d'Angely, 2 June 1453, and sends Joachim Rouault to retake Chalais.

16 French army moves towards Dordogne Valley, start of June 1453.

17 French (supposedly from de Clermont's army but more likely from Foix's army) retake Saint-Sauveur-le-Vicomte, probably from a local Gascon lord who had declared for the English regime, start of June 1453.

18 French army under Jean de Clermont advances across the Bazadais and Bordelais regions, meeting no resistance, penetrating the Médoc region, June 1453.

19 French army under Count of Foix marches north in close cooperation with de Clermont's army.

20 Joachim Rouault attacks Chalais, 14 June 1453.

21 Chalais falls to assault, 21 June 1453.

22 Anglo-Gascon relief force turns back to Bordeaux, 21 June 1453.

23 Jean de Clermont receives a letter from Talbot dated 21 June 1453, requesting that the French cause no damage as the Anglo-Gascons are offering no resistance.

24 French armies of de Clermont and Foix join forces to occupy Martignas, around 24 June 1453; de Clermont requests a 'meeting' (in battle) with Talbot 'in three days' time', around 25 June 1453; Talbot agrees under certain conditions.

25 Learning that the armies of de Clermont and Foix have united, Talbot retreats to Bordeaux; the French pursue, destroying a unit of archers around 25 June 1453.

26 Joachim Rouault's force joins the French now under Jean de Bueil, etc., late June 1453.

27 Fleet consisting of French and other hired ships from Holland, Zealand, Flanders, Brittany, Poitou and Spain assembles at La Rochelle under the Admiral of Brittany, summer 1453.

28 Part of Jean de Bueil's army under Louis de Beaumont Saint-Jean d'Angély takes Gensac, 8 July 1453.

29 French army under Jean de Bueil crosses the Dordogne to besiege Castillon, 9–10 July; the rest probably recrosses the river at Sante-Foy-la-Grande, then marches down the northern bank towards Castillon.

30 Gaston de l'Isle surrenders Castelnau to de Clermont's army, which then besieges nearby Châteauneuf-de-Médoc, 14 July 1453; French also ravage area to deny supplies to Bordeaux.

31 De Clermont attempts to take Bordeaux by surprise but fails; a regular siege is established, mid-July 1453.

32 Count of Foix separates from de Clermont to ravage the Bas-Médoc area, mid-July 1453.

33 Anglo-Gascon army under Talbot marches from Bordeaux to Libourne and past Saint-Émilion to Castillon, 16–17 July 1453.

34 Anglo-Gascon army defeated at battle of Castillon, 17 July 1453; French cavalry under Count of Pontièvre pursues fugitives to Saint-Émilion; Castillon surrenders to French following artillery bombardment, 18–20 July 1453.

35 Charles VII takes his army to Angoulême, 17 July 1453.

36 French march to besiege Cadillac, 18 July 1453.

37 Anglo-Gascon survivors of Castillon assemble in Bordeaux; Roger de Camoys, as the new Seneschal of Guyenne, attempts to send reinforcements to Rions, Libourne, Cadillac and Blanquefort, 18–20 July 1453.

38 Charles VII goes to La Rochefoucault and orders an investigation into the taking of Castillon, 22–24 July 1453.

39 Charles VII decides that his presence is necessary to maintain discipline, 28 July 1453; he reaches Abbey of La Couronne, 30 July 1453.

40 Charles VII's army joins the siege of Libourne, where Charles arranges the settlement's surrender, and then leads his army and that of de Clermont to besiege Fronsac, 8 August 1453.

41 Anglo-Gascon relief force under the Sire of Anglade heads for Fronsac but turns back on hearing of its surrender, around 10 August 1453.

42 Châteauneuf and Blanquefort surrender, 29 July 1453.

43 Saint-Émilion surrenders and Libourne is besieged, end of June 1453.

44 Charles VII crosses the Dordogne to establish his headquarters at Montferrant, 13 August 1453; part of the French army encamps at Lormont while another part, including siege troops under Jean Bureau, strengthens Count of Foix's siege of Cadillac.

45 Parts of the army besieging Cadillac are detached to take Saint-Macaire, Langon and Villandraut, 13 August 1453.

46 French fleet moves from La Rochelle to Lormont, September 1453; under nominal command of Jean Bueil, it blockades Bordeaux, late September or early October 1453.

47 Final payment to Anglo-Gascon garrison of Cadillac, 17 September 1453; Cadillac surrenders a few days later.

48 Epidemic breaks out in French army besieging Bordeaux and in the city a short while later; negotiations at Lormont from 5–9 October 1453; Anglo-Gascon hostages handed over, outer fortifications surrendered, gates of Bordeaux opened 10–16 October 1453; official capitulation of Bordeaux on 17 October 1453; English garrison departs 'in full honour' but Charles VII leaves for Poitiers rather than ceremonially entering the city, 19 October 1453.

49 Pro-English Gascon garrisons of Bénauges and Rions surrender, late October 1453.

The final phase of the French conquest of Gascony 1452–53

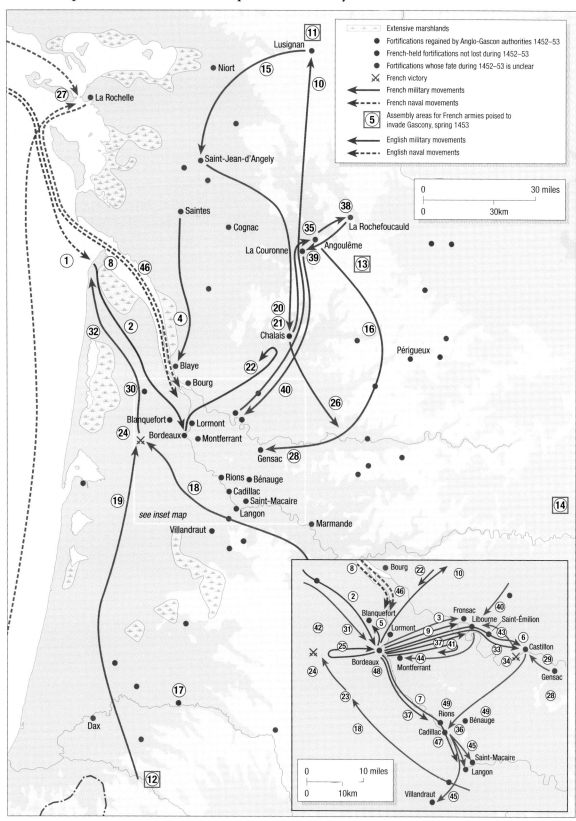

Extensive marshlands

● Fortifications regained by Anglo-Gascon authorities 1452–53

● French-held fortifications not lost during 1452–53

● Fortifications whose fate during 1452–53 is unclear

✕ French victory

→ French military movements

⇢ French naval movements

⑤ Assembly areas for French armies poised to invade Gascony, spring 1453

← English military movements

⇠ English naval movements

0   30 miles
0   30km

Lusignan

Niort

La Rochelle

Saint-Jean-d'Angely

Saintes

Cognac

La Rochefoucauld

La Couronne

Angoulême

Chalais

Périgueux

Blaye

Bourg

Blanquefort

Lormont

Bordeaux

Montferrant

Gensac

Rions

Bénauge

Cadillac

Saint-Macaire

Langon

Villandraut

Marmande

Dax

see inset map

Inset map

Bourg

Blanquefort

Lormont

Fronsac

Libourne

Saint-Émilion

Bordeaux

Montferrant

Castillon

Gensac

Rions

Cadillac

Bénauge

Saint-Macaire

Langon

Villandraut

0   10 miles
0   10km

army would also spread to Bordeaux, though it is unclear whether this happened before or after the city finally capitulated.

On the other side, the French built a huge *bastille* next to the shore at Lormont to serve as an artillery position to defend Lormont's river harbour and command part of the river. After the fall of Cadillac, Jean Bureau directed an artillery force of some 250 cannon of various sizes, all trained on the defences of Bordeaux or the river. Meanwhile, Jean de Bueil was given the title of 'Lieutenant of the Sea and the Land for the Gironde'. For his part, Charles VII set about assembling a large fleet, hiring or commandeering ships from Holland, Zealand, Flanders, Brittany, Poitou and Spain, all 'armed and victualled'. The captains of the Spanish ships are known to have been paid 9,000 livres. Their vessels and the others gathered at the recently strengthened fortified port of La Rochelle under the Admiral of Brittany.

This fleet then moved to Lormont on the east bank of the Garonne, facing Bordeaux, where Jean de Bueil took over as nominal commander, though the Admiral of Brittany remained in operational command. Its primary purpose was to stop food supplies, mainly of wheat and mostly from Bristol, from reaching Bordeaux from England. Meanwhile, the English tried to assemble a relief fleet commanded by Lord Say, but it could not set sail in time and would probably not have been able to break through to Bordeaux even if it had.

In August 1453 the English government declared that King Henry VI had relapsed into madness after hearing news of the English collapse in Gascony. Edmund Beaufort's influence was restored at court and Queen Margaret's supporters were strengthened by the news that she was pregnant. Meanwhile, the Duke of York found himself politically isolated once again. Efforts to organize another military expedition to relieve Bordeaux achieved virtually nothing and it seemed as if England, if not yet the English court, had given up. It is perhaps significant that the entry for 1453 in the *London Chronicle* made no mention of foreign affairs at all.

Away in Gascony it was probably the French fleet, now based at Lormont, that finally brought Anglo-Gascon Bordeaux to its knees. During the final weeks of the siege it may have been preparing to attack the Anglo-Gascon vessels outside the city, but in the event this was not needed. Charles VII offered safe conduct to enemy representatives and the city council of Bordeaux eventually agreed to negotiate, though active hostilities still continued. On 5 October a delegation led by Roger de Camoys crossed the river to Lormont, where it was received by Admiral Jean de Bueil as King Charles VII's representative, accompanied by Jean d'Estouteville, Louis de Beaumont-Bressuire and Jean de Chambes. This first meeting and another the following day seemed to achieve nothing, with Roger de Camoys insisting that the English, their ships and their goods all be allowed to return unhindered to England.

Both sides were, of course, testing each other's resolve, and on 8 October an agreement was signed whereby the *bastille* of Bordeaux would be handed over to the French, along with all prisoners in English hands. The following day Roger de Camoys and eight to ten of the leading citizens of Bordeaux went to the castle of Montferrant, where they met Charles VII himself. Charles could make concessions that were not allowed to his representatives, and he now granted an amnesty for the leaders of Gascony and Bordeaux, whom the French had declared to be traitors. Some 20 of the most senior were, nevertheless, excluded, including the lords of Lesparre and Duras. Negotiations continued, and Roger de Camoys eventually got Charles to agree that these 20 should be banished rather than executed.

On 12 October six English and six Gascon hostages were handed over as a guarantee that the agreements would be honoured. Two days later further hostages were handed over, along with the *bastille*. Two days after that the gates of Bordeaux were opened. From 16–18 October the English were allowed to settle their affairs in Bordeaux, and on 19 October French banners were raised over the city. The English garrison departed 'in full honour' and Charles VII give each man an *écu*, while sending his own troops and heralds to ensure that the men boarded their ships without interference from the French.

The English had left Gascony, but the castles of Rions and Bénauges were still held by Gascon lords who had yet to submit to Charles VII. Once they had been blockaded and forced to surrender, the Hundred Years War was truly over. Even so, many French leaders wanted Bordeaux to suffer for inviting the English back. Charles VII disagreed and decided that mercy would be a more effective method of integrating these long-separated areas into a unified French kingdom. He ordered that Bordeaux's battered fortifications be repaired and that two new citadels be erected: the Fortress of Hâ and the Castle of Trompette, both of which would be demolished early in the 19th century. As for himself, Charles decided not to make a formal entry into the conquered city but instead went back to the Poitou region. Thereafter, he never again marched at the head of his troops on an active campaign.

AFTERMATH

THE IMPACT ON FRANCE

The most significant long-term impact that victory in these final campaigns had upon France was to strengthen the prestige and centralizing power of the French monarchy. Some historians have even suggested that it set France on the road to absolute monarchy because the majority of the people believed, with some justification, that the country's survival as an independent state had been down to the skill and persistence of a strong ruler.

Charles VII had wisely avoided the temptation to punish areas or towns that were considered to have supported the English. On the other hand he did reward those that could claim to have been faithful. One such was Bayonne, in the far south-western corner of the country, which, having been taken for the French king in the late 1440s, had not allowed itself to be retaken by the English or their local Gascon allies. Charles also recognized the need for national reconciliation if he was to achieve national unity in the wake of the Hundred Years War. This posed considerable problems in those areas where most of the people had obeyed an English ruler as if he had been the lawful king of France. Charles VII therefore insisted that matters be dealt with through a recognized legal process, which, though it may in many ways have been a sham, did enable him to then graciously 'remit and pardon' those found guilty. It also enhanced his reputation as a caring rather than vengeful monarch.

There were, of course, significant trials, some of which involved men who had played a significant role in those final campaigns. One of these was the Duke of Alençon, who was accused of plotting to help the English return to Normandy after the war was over. He was tried at Vendôme in September 1458, where another very senior French nobleman, Charles of Orléans, spoke in his defence, pointing out to the King that, 'for a long time past none of your predecessors has held the kingdom so united in his grasp as you hold it now'. Apart from being a plea for mercy, it was also a recognition of the success of the King's policy of reconciliation. The Duke of Alençon was found guilty, but he was treated with remarkable leniency considering the gravity of the charge of treason. Charles VII's reputation for clemency thus received another boost, as it did following similar trials in Gascony.

Local celebrations, festivals and special religious services to commemorate the victorious conclusion of the Hundred Years War remained a feature of Normandy and Gascony until the French Revolution, when events marking French 'royal' successes were banned. Thereafter, and throughout the

19th century, these victories – especially those in Normandy – were used to raise local French patriotism. New monuments were erected on several battlefields, notably Formigny and Castillon, while the period of English rule in Normandy was presented as a time of harsh, alien occupation. Only in the later 19th century did French historians produce more balanced and moderate interpretations of the period, though even then the underlying anti-English tone did not disappear until the Anglo-French Entente Cordiale of the early 20th century. World War I, World War II and especially D-Day and the liberation of 1944 finally removed the last traces of resentful xenophobia.

Back in the second half of the 15th century, the end of the Hundred Years War led to widespread hopes that the King's expensive and not always well-disciplined army would be dismissed. This did not happen, and frequent demands from various parts of France to have their local garrisons reduced in order to cut costs were only occasionally satisfied. One of those areas that did see a reduction in 1451, following the Normandy campaign, was the Auvergne. Even so, there were two sides to the coin: while garrisons could be a major burden on the local economy, they could also form a source of revenue and trade.

At the same time there was now widespread pride in France and in the achievements of the French army. This was clearly reflected in a popular tale called 'The Debate between the Heralds of France and England', in which the English were portrayed as a people who knew how to start a war, while the French were portrayed as a people who knew how to end it. For many decades this pride in the French military was entirely justified, especially where French artillery was concerned. What has been called the gunpowder revolution had only just started, and would be a feature of 16th- rather than 15th-century warfare. Nevertheless, guns were already having a significant impact, despite being cumbersome, small in number and having a very slow

One of the most interesting 15th-century gargoyles on St Mary Magdalene Church in the village of Battlefield, near Shrewsbury, shows an armoured man loading a cannon. (Author's photograph)

rate of fire. In siege warfare the mere appearance of the French artillery train had often been enough to convince a garrison to submit. Here it is worth noting that changes in the design of most fortifications remained limited and localized. Indeed, until around 1530 existing castles and urban defences were largely at the mercy of increasingly effective siege artillery. This would also be a period characterized by large numbers of significant field battles. In fact, by the end of the 15th century, French artillery, including what could now correctly be called field guns, was advanced and effective enough to surprise many Italian observers (see Campaign 43: *Fornovo 1495*, Osprey Publishing Ltd: Oxford, 1996).

A number of the men who had distinguished themselves in the Normandy or Gascony campaigns continued to serve with distinction. Amongst those of middle rank, Joachim Rouault served Charles VII and his son Louis XI, fighting for the King against the Duke of Burgundy. Later he found himself in trouble and was even sentenced to banishment, though the sentence was not carried out. Indeed, when Joachim Rouault died in 1478 he was still in possession of considerable land and wealth, and was buried in the Church of the Cordeliers in Thouars. There is very little to indicate that many of the Scottish mercenaries who fought for Charles VII ever went home. Most of those who survived seem to have integrated into French society and married locally. To quote B. Ditcham: 'Certainly by 1460, the foreigners who were in the French armies mostly belonged nowhere else but in France.' Here, he pointed out, they formed the first large group of immigrant workers in French society.[14] How far this was also true of the Spanish, Italian and German mercenaries is less clear.

An unknown number of English soldiers from the defeated armies also remained in France, though a handful of names are known. One such was Sir Richard Merbury, who had married a French woman and who now took the oath of allegiance to the French Crown, eventually becoming a counsellor and chamberlain to Charles VII. The Welsh captain John Edwards, who had surrendered the castle of Roche-Guyon, similarly had a French wife and now

14 Ditcham, B., *The Employment of Foreign Mercenary Troops in the French Royal Armies, 1415–1470* (Ph.D. thesis, Edinburgh University, 1979) p. 309.

swore allegiance to King Charles. Others included Peter and Tassin Damport, John Marbury and John Basset. A certain Walter Stokely had been part of the Falaise garrison when the castle surrendered in 1450 and was still residing in the town three years later. The number of non-military men and their families who stayed behind was almost certainly greater; several fully assimilated families later took pride in their descent from the 'English of England'. Even today many historians see the flourishing Bordeaux wine trade as a heritage of the medieval link between England and Gascony.

At the time, of course, the economic aftermath of the war was less straightforward, with both English and French sources describing much of Normandy and France as far south as the river Loire as being depopulated and devastated for years after the war ended. This was also the case around Bordeaux, and resulted in the French government trying to attract new people to resettle these areas. On the other hand, the belief that the economy of Normandy had suffered badly under English rule seems exaggerated; the ability of the area to flourish within a decade or so suggests that not much physical damage had been done to its infrastructure during the occupation or the reconquest. Indeed, some areas benefited from changes in patterns of life and trade; one such being Pont-Audemer in Normandy, which became a major fishing port, particularly for herrings, after 1450.

The French authorities continued to fear an English attempt to regain Normandy, and there was still a certain degree of pro-English sentiment in some areas. One of the main sources of friction concerned the competing rights of the 'exiles' or loyalists who had left Normandy rather than live under English rule, and those who were now in possession of land and property.

The effigy of Robert Hungerford, who died in 1459, shows the very latest and most sophisticated style of armour used in England during this period; his son was captured at the battle of Castillon and is also buried in Salisbury Cathedral. (*In situ* Salisbury Cathedral; Antoinette Nicolle photograph)

Eventually Charles VII proclaimed the Edict of Compiègne, which generally declared in favour of exiled loyalists, though the matter was further complicated by the fact that some of these families did not want to return to areas damaged by war. There were also problems with institutions such as the University of Caen, which had been founded under English rule in 1432, and with an urban merchant middle class which had flourished through trade with England and beyond.

These feelings probably did not reflect any lingering desire on the part of the Norman population to be ruled from England. Indeed, by the 15th century Normandy had lost the separate and somewhat warlike identity that had existed in the 11th and 12th centuries. Instead it was now a peaceful, fertile and prosperous but otherwise quite typical French province. Indeed, for many years its people took pride in being notably loyal to the French Crown, though they remained very attached to their local traditions, distinctive Norman-French dialect and a tendency to react strongly against any hint of tyranny – characteristics that would endure through the following centuries. Meanwhile, the Duchy of Normandy remained in existence as a distinct entity until 9 November 1469, when the old Ducal seal was broken as a sign that the land of Normandy was now incorporated within the royal domain of France.

Circumstances and attitudes were very different in Gascony, where the sense of being different from the rest of France went much deeper and had a longer history. Most of the 20 men whom Charles VII had insisted leave the country had gone to England, though the Captal de Buch moved to the neighbouring Kingdom of Aragon, where he owned land. Some of them could not accept that the struggle was over, amongst them Pierre de Montferrant, the Lord of Lesparre, who returned secretly in 1454. Captured and accused of trying to 'stir up enmity to the French' he could hope for no mercy this time, and was executed. This seems to have been the last serious attempt to regain Gascon independence, though a highly distinctive Gascon regional identity survives to this day.

THE IMPACT ON ENGLAND

The impact within England of having lost a war that had gone on for almost a century was of course considerable, though at first it was largely political. The fall of Normandy in 1449 and even more so the failure to regain it in 1450 undermined a government dominated by the Duke of Suffolk. It also fatally undermined what remained of King Henry VI's authority because the monarch seemed unable to bring himself to act decisively. The King's fragile mental health had been a major factor in English politics for several years and his new decline proved to be a slow-burning rather than an immediate crisis. With the fall of the Duke of Suffolk, the Duke of York once more became the 'Protector' of England in 1454. The following year a real crisis erupted with the first clashes of the Wars of the Roses – a civil conflict that would end only when Henry Tudor seized the throne in 1485 as King Henry VII. By then, of course, Henry VI had been deposed in 1461, restored to the throne in 1470 and finally murdered in the Tower of London in 1471.

For reasons that are still difficult to understand, this notably ineffective monarch came to be venerated in England as a royal saint, and remained so until King Henry VIII broke with Rome to establish the superficially Protestant Church of England. Henry VI's reign had witnessed a whole series of disasters,

One of the 15th-century swords found a few years ago in the river Dordogne, next to the battlefield of Castillon. (Private collection)

England's last toehold: the Pale of Calais

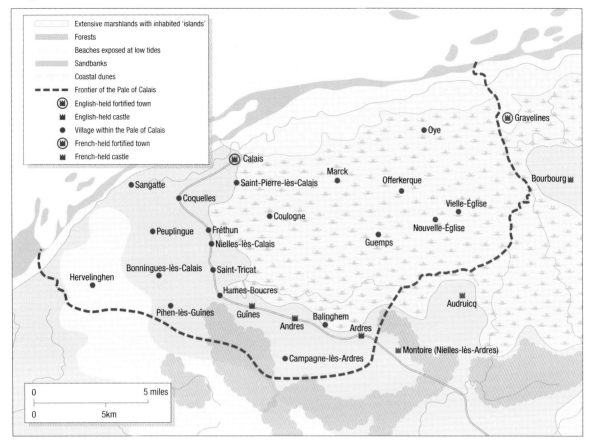

both in France and at home, and was followed by the similarly disastrous Wars of the Roses. Nevertheless, his cult as a saint proved particularly popular in London and in the royal town of Windsor, though it was also seen elsewhere. The King himself was regarded as a man of suffering who was pious and attempted to do good in a wicked world. Henry VI was even credited with being responsible for miracles, especially the healing of children and the curing of those suffering from 'plague' – a term which then covered a number of different diseases. Amongst the educated he was also remembered, correctly, as an important cultural figure who promoted learning.

Lower down the social scale, failure in the Hundred Years Wars caused problems for a wide variety of individuals and families. This was particularly true of those who had taken an active part in the final disastrous campaigns, not only commanders but middle-ranking men and ordinary soldiers. In the words of an acknowledged expert in this field, Anne Curry: 'The "investment level" of the soldiering classes was no less great [than that of the English government]. It is easy to see, therefore, that many must have returned to England… disappointed, disillusioned and disgruntled'.[15] In 1452 the government is known to have received a petition from men who had lost possessions in Maine and Normandy, informing the King that, 'at present

---

15 Curry, A., 'English Armies in the Fifteenth Century' in A. Curry and M. Hughes (eds.), *Arms, Armies and Fortifications in the Hundred Years War* (Woodbridge, 1994) p. 68.

most of them are completely ruined and reduced to beggary, which is a sad matter, given the good and just right you have to the said country'. Some of the returning soldiers were unwilling to just wait until they were offered support, many reportedly being in a state of near-mutiny. Others who fled from Normandy or Gascony were not immediately welcomed as Englishmen, many having to acquire 'letters of denization'. This was a method under English common law whereby a foreigner started the process of becoming an English subject. It was used until the second half of the 19th century.

Some established aristocratic families faced equally immediate though different problems, usually arising from the need to raise large sums of money to pay the ransoms of captured relatives. This could be devastating, even for wealthy and powerful families, and some men remained prisoners in France for many years. For example, Thomas Kyriell returned to England quite soon but his unfortunate brother John was still held in France in 1470.

Amongst those noblemen captured at Castillon was Robert Hungerford Lord Moleyns, whose ransom was initially set at £6,000 and was then raised to £9,800 – a staggering sum for the period. As a result, his family were obliged to sell or mortgage their property on a massive scale, the debt remaining a source of financial, social and political embarrassment for Moleyns and his kinsmen for years, even after his eventual release. Even so, they avoided making use of professional financiers as far as was possible; instead relying upon friends and neighbours. The matter was made yet more complicated for the Moleyns family by Robert Hungerford's loyalty to the Lancastrian cause during the Wars of the Roses, resulting in his execution in 1464. The ransoms of lower-ranking prisoners were of course lower, but were often beyond their families' ability to pay. A man named John Swan was captured at the battle of Formigny in 1450 and was taken to the town of Carentan. There he was recorded pleading for alms, 'else he must needs be sworn French or utterly die'.

Defeat also prompted some men to write books, which they hoped would raise both the morale and the effectiveness of English armies. One such was William Worcester. He had personal experience of the war against the French, having served in France under Sir John Fastolf, and his work was full of strident nationalism. Entitled the *Boke of Noblesse*, it was probably written in the 1450s in the hope that King Henry VI would adopt his father Henry V's aggressive policies in France. With the fall of the Lancastrian dynasty, the text was modified to appeal to the new Yorkist ruler, King Edward IV, and was presented to him as he was about to set off on a notably unsuccessful campaign in France. William Worcester even went so far as to blame the current problems in England on the fact that the kingdom was at peace with its old enemy, France. He also seems to have been more upset by the loss of Normandy than of Bordeaux, regarding it as a particularly damaging blow to England's prestige.

Defeat in the Hundred Years War did not, however, seem to have much impact upon England's relations with other countries, though the subsequent civil war – the Wars of the Roses – did expose the kingdom to outside interference. Interestingly enough, one of the country's old foes, Joachim Rouault, was sent on an embassy to England in 1456 to support the Lancastrians against the Yorkists. England was also deeply worried about the possibility of a French invasion, being understandably concerned that the enemy might try to 'get their own back'. In 1457 French fleets did indeed attack the southern English ports of Sandwich and Fowey. Nevertheless it is important to understand that it was not England's failure in the Hundred Years War that made the country turn away from Europe and look towards a wider world across the oceans. That came much later and stemmed from the growing sense of cultural isolationism that arose out of the English Reformation and the break with the Church of Rome.

POSTSCRIPT IN CALAIS

The defeat of the Duke of Burgundy's assault upon English-held Calais in 1436 is sometimes dismissed as a sideshow in the wider affairs of the Hundred Years War. In fact it was a major setback for the Burgundians, Calais being within their zone of military responsibility. There was fear that the Burgundians would return once Normandy was lost in 1450, but negotiations with the Duke resulted in extended truces. From then on the Pale of Calais was all that remained of English possessions in northern France, apart from the Channel Islands.

Somehow some remnants of Talbot's defeated army made their way to Calais following the battle of Castillon, though how they did so remains a mystery. They are more likely to have stopped off while sailing home from Bordeaux. Most such troops continued to England, but some are known to have joined the Calais garrison. Indeed, service in Calais would have remained a prestigious position, especially for senior officers.

On the other hand the seemingly declining rank of those who served as Captain of Calais might suggest that it came to be seen as a place for professional soldiers rather than ambitious nobles. In 1451 the Duke of Buckingham was followed by the Count of Wiltshire; then came the Viscount of Berkshire, the Lord of Sudely, followed by a sequence of knights: John of Stourton, Thomas Stanleye and Thomas Rempston. Calais then started to play a role in the Wars of the Roses, sometimes as a jumping-off point for invasions by forces opposed to the current ruler, sometimes as a place of refuge for those currently out of favour at court. Thus the aristocratic rank of the captaincy rose once more, with Count Richard Nevill of Warwick being appointed in 1455 following the battle of St Albans. He then remained in the post through the first ten years of Edward IV's reign.[16]

Calais had been turned into an almost exclusively English town after its conquest by Edward III at the start of the Hundred Years War and now, not surprisingly, the French authorities feared it as a centre of intelligence-gathering and subversion. The situation only really stabilized in 1475, with the signing of the Truce of Picquigny. This was intended to last for nine years, but in truth it marked the real end of the Hundred Years War. Otherwise, there was no official end to that prolonged conflict, and English monarchs maintained their increasingly irrelevant claim to the French throne until the Napoleonic wars. The fleurs-de-lis of France were then finally removed from the royal coat of arms in 1801, by which time, of course, the exclave of Calais had been lost, falling to a sudden French assault in 1558.

---

16 Richard Turpyn (attrib.) (ed. J.G. Nichols), *The Chronicle of Calais* (London, 1846) p. xxxvii.

THE BATTLEFIELDS TODAY

The Priory of Saint-Florent no longer exists, but some carved capitals and perhaps an arch might have been incorporated into the nearby Protestant church, which was built around the same time that the old priory was replaced by Castillon's railway station. (Author's photograph)

These campaigns of 1449–53 ranged over such a wide area that the following comments will focus only on the main battlefields of Formigny and Castillon. Both are easily accessible because these battles were fought on major medieval roads, which remain major arteries today. Being in France, the localities are also well served with hotels, campsites, restaurants, bars and, to a rather lesser extent, public transport. At the time of the author's visit a few years ago there was an excellent Logis de France bed-and-breakfast hotel at Trévières and somewhat simpler *gîte* guest houses in Engranville and several other nearby villages.

The village of Formigny is used to foreign visitors, though the overwhelming majority come to visit the nearby D-Day landing beaches. Apart from a dramatic 19th-century bronze monument to celebrate the French victory in 1450, the site of the battle is also marked by a simple chapel, built in 1486 on the orders of de Clermont, who was by then better known as Duke Jean II of Bourbon. It stands next to the bridge that was such a vital feature in the events of 15 April 1450. For many years a number of relics from the battlefield were stored in a chest in this chapel, including bullets and the skeleton of a man still wearing a mail shirt; the shirt is now on show at the Musée de Normandie in Caen. A local doctor also dug up a medieval sword on the battlefield in 1813. Three years later he gave it to the Duke of Aumont, whose ancestor had taken part in the battle of Formigny, but unfortunately the sword's present whereabouts are unknown.

The battlefield of Castillon is marked by two monuments. A modern one overlooking the site from the north is dedicated to Jean Bureau, to whom most historians now give primary credit for the French victory. The other, marking the site where John Talbot was killed, is at the southern edge of the battlefield, and although it has been altered over the years it is the older of the two. Still known as the Talbot Monument, it highlights the admiration French contemporaries and indeed present-day Frenchmen still have for a warrior of whom Matthew d'Escoucy wrote: 'Such was the end of this famous and renowned English leader who for so long had been one of the most formidable thorns in the side of the French, who regarded him with terror and dismay.'

FURTHER READING

(anon. ed.), *La 'France Anglaise' au Moyen Age* (Paris, 1988) several articles

Allmand, C. T., 'Changing Views of the Soldier in Late Medieval France' in Contamine, P., (et al. eds.), *Guerre et Société en France, en Angleterre et en Bourgogne, XIVe et XVe siècle* (Lille 1991) pp. 171–188

Allmand, C. T., and M. Keen, 'History and the Literature of War; The Boke of Noblesse of William Worcester' in C. T. Alland (ed.), *War, Government and Power in Late Medieval France* (Liverpool, 2000) pp. 92–105

Allmand, C. T., *Lancastrian Normandy, 1415–1450, The History of a Medieval Occupation* (Oxford, 1983)

Allmand, C. T. (ed.), *War, Literature and Politics in the Late Middle Ages* (Liverpool, 1976) several articles

Barthe, J., *La victoire de Castillon* (1977)

Basin, Thomas (ed. and tr. C. Samaran), *Histoire de Charles VII, tome 2, 1445–1461* (Paris, 1965)

Battesti, M., *Castillon: La fin d'un monde; Historia Special*, 55 (Paris, September–October 1998)

Bully, P., *Charles VII le 'roi des merveilles'* (Paris, 1994)

Burne, A. H., 'The Battle of Castillon, 1453; the end of the Hundred Years War' in *History Today* (April, 1953) pp. 249–56

——, 'The French Camp at Castillon' in *Royal Engineers Journal* (1948) pp. 290–91

——, *The Agincourt War: A military history of the latter part of the Hundred Years War from 1369 to 1453* (London, 1956)

Chartier, Jean and Alain (ed. V. de Viriville), *Chronique de Charles VII, Roi de France, tome II* (Paris, 1858)

Christie, M. B., *Henry VI* (London, 1922)

Contamine, P., 'The Soldiery in Late Medieval Society' in *French History*, 8 (1994) pp. 1–13

——, *Guerre, Etat et Société à la Fin du Moyen Age: Etudes sur les armées des rois de France 1337–1494* (Paris, 1972)

——, *Histoire militaire de la France, vol. 1* (Paris, 1992)

Cosneau, E., *Le Connétable De Richement (Arthur de Bretagne) (1393–1458)* (Paris, 1886)

Craig, L. A., 'Royalty, Virtue, and Adversity: The Cult of King Henry VI' in *Albion*, 35 (2003) pp. 187–209

Curry. A. E., 'The Impact of War and Occupation on Urban Life in Normandy, 1417–1450' in *French History*, 1 (1987) pp. 157–81

——, 'The Nationality of Men-at-Arms Serving in English Armies in Normandy and the *pays de conquête* (1415–1450)' in *Reading Medieval Studies*, 18 (1992) pp. 135–63

Curry, A., and Hughes, M. (eds.), *Arms, Armies and Fortifications in the Hundred Years War* (Woodbridge, 1994) several articles

Curry, A., and Matthew, E. (eds.), *Concepts and Patterns of Service in the Late Middle Ages* (Woodbridge, 2000) several articles

De Belleval, *Du Costume Militaire des Français en 1446* (Paris, 1866)

De Bueil, Jean (introduction and ed. L. Lecestre), *Le Jouvencel par Jean de Bueil* (Paris, 1887)

Ditcham, B. G. H., *The Employment of Foreign Mercenary Troops in the French Royal Armies, 1415–1470* (PhD thesis Edinburgh University, 1979)

——, '"Mutton Guzzlers and Wine Bags"; Foreign Soldiers and Native Reactions in Fifteenth-Century France' in C. Allmand (ed.), *Power, Culture and Religion in France, c.1350–c.1550* (Woodbridge, 1989) pp. 1–13

Drouyn, L., *La Guyenne Militaire* (Paris, 1865)

Du Fresne du Beaucourt, G., *Histoire de Charles VII, tome V: Le Roi Victorieux 1449–1453* (Paris, 1890)

Evans, M. R., 'Brigandage and Resistance in Lancastrian Normandy' in *Reading Medieval Studies*, 18 (1992) pp. 103–33

Fieffé, E., *Histoire des Troupes Etrangères au service de France* (Paris, 1854)

Goldmann, C., 'Le Roi à la Guerre; L'oeuvre méconnue de Charles VII' in *Histoire et Images Médiévales*, 8 (June–July, 2006) pp. 30–53

Griffiths, R. A., *The Reign of King Henry VI: The exercise of royal authority, 1422–1461* (1998)

Gruel, Guillaume (A. Le Vavasseur ed.), *Chronique d'Arthur de Richemont, Connétable de France, Duc de Bretagne (1393–1458)* (Paris, 1890)

Guignard, F., *Histoire de Castillon-sur-Dordogne* (Paris, 1912, reprinted Castillon, 2003)

Joret, C., *La Bataille de Formigny d'après les documents contemporains* (Paris, 1903)

Keen, M., 'The End of the Hundred Years War: Lancastrian France and Lancastrian England' in M. Jones and M. Vale (eds.), *England and Her Neighbours, 1066–1453* (London, 1989) pp. 297–311

Kerhervé, J., 'Arthur de Richemont, connétable et duc: Entre guerre et politique, dans la France du XVe siècle' (anon ed.) in *2000 ans d'histoire de Vannes* (Archives municipales de Vannes: Vannes, 1993) pp. 95–120

Kilgour, R. L., *The Decline of Chivalry as shown in the French Literature of the Late Middle Ages* (Gloucester, MA, 1966)

Labarge, M. W., *Gascony: England's First Colony 1204–1453* (1980)

Le Bouvier, Gilles (Le Hérault Berry) (ed. H. Courteault and L. Celier), *Les Chroniques du Roi Charles VII* (Paris, 1979)

Lodge, E. C., *Gascony under English Rule* (London, 1926)

Lot, F., *L'Art Militaire et les Armées au Moyen Age* (Paris, 1946)

Marillier, B., 'La bataille de Castillon' in *Histoire et Images Médiévales*, 2 (June–July, 2005) pp. 6–67

Marin, J-Y. (ed.), *La Normandie dans la guerre de Cent Ans, 1346–1450* (Caen, 1999) several articles

Nicholson, J. L., 'The French Camp at Castillon' in *Royal Engineers Journal* (1949) pp. 156–58

Oakeshott, E., 'The Swords of Castillon' in *Park Lane Arms Fair*, 10 (1993) pp. 7–16

Pollard, A. J., *John Talbot and the War in France, 1427–1453* (1983)

Richebé, J. (et al. eds.), *Les Plus Anciens Récits de la Bataille de Castillon* (Castillon, n.d.)

Solon, P. D., 'Popular Response to Standing Armies in Fifteenth-century France' in *Studies in the Renaissance*, 19 (1972) pp. 78–111

——, 'Valois Military Administration on the Norman Frontier, 1445–1461,' in *Speculum*, 51 (1976) pp. 91–111

Spont, A., 'La Milice des Francs-Archers (1448–1500)' in *Revue des Questions Historiques*, 59 (1897) pp. 441–89

Stevenson, J. (ed.), *Narratives of the Expulsion of the English from Normandy* (1863)

Talbot, H., *The English Achilles: The Life and Campaigns of John Talbot, 1st Earl of Shrewsbury* (1981)

Thibault, J., 'Un Prince Territorial au XVe siècle, Dunois, Bâtard d'Orléans' in *Bulletin de la Société Archéologique et Historique de l'Orléans*, 14 (1997) pp. 3–46

Trévédy, J-T-M., 'La bataille de Formigny (15 avril 1450)' in *Bulletin de la Société Archéologique de Finisterre*, 30 (1903) pp. 241–75

Vale, M. G. A., *Charles VII* (1974)

——, *English Gascony 1399–1453* (Oxford, 1970)

——, *War and chivalry: warfare and aristocratic culture in England, France and Burgundy at the end of the Middle Ages* (London, 1981)

Watts, J., *Henry VI and the politics of kingship* (1996)

Williams, A. R., 'Some firing tests with simulated fifteenth-century handguns' in *Journal of the Arms and Armour Society*, 8 (1974) pp. 114–20

Wolff, B, *Henry VI* (London, 1981)

INDEX

References to illustrations are shown in **bold**. Plates are shown with page in **bold** and caption in brackets, e.g. **32-33** (34).

Agincourt, battle of (1415) 5, 13, 18, 21
Aidie, Odet d' 29
Albret, Lord of 49, 77
Alençon 23
Alengour, Hélix 38
'Allegory of Blind Death' **17**
Allmand, C.T. 67
Anglade, Lord of 51, 72
Anglo-Burgundian alliance (1416) 5, 7, 18
Angoulême 51, 74
armour **14**, **16**, **39**, **73**, **77**, **87**
    see also tabards
Arpel, Jean 38
Aubercon, Christofle (also known as
    Auberchon) 35
Auvergne, Martial d' **12**, 59, 71–72
Avranches 38
Ayscough, William, Bishop of Salisbury 41

Basceler, Janequin (also known as Basquier
    or Pasquier) 38
Basel 10
Basin, Thomas 28, 46, 63, 67, 70, 71
Bayeux **25**, 26–27, **27**, 29, 30, 35, 38
Bayonne 6, 25, 42, 84
Beaumont-Bressuire, Louis (II) de 49, 51, 82
Beauvau, Pierre de, Lord of Bessière 49, 51,
    61, 72, 77
Bec, Arnaud 46
Blanquefort 75, 77, 79–80
Bordeaux **47**, **78**
    conquered by the French (1451) 42–43
    retaken by the English 45–48, 50–51,
        59–60, 75–77
    siege (1453) 74, 79–80, 82–83
    see also Gascony
Bourges 5, 18, **45**
Boussac, Lord of 51
Brézé, Pierre de **14**, 22–23, 31, 35
Bridge of Meulan 21
Brittany 6, 7, 22
    see also François I, Duke of Brittany;
        Pierre II, Duke of Brittany
Brutails, Louis de 45–46
Bureau, Gaspard 11, **17**, 19, 59
Bureau, Jean 11, **17**, 19
    Gascony campaign (Castillon) 51, 54–55,
        59, 72, 92
    Gascony campaign (end of) 74, 75,
        77, 82
    Normandy campaign 39
Burgundy 5, 6, 7, 18, **49**, 91
    see also Duke of Burgundy
Burne, A. H. 63

Cadillac, siege of 75, 76, 77, 79, 82
Caen 26–27, 28, 35, 38–39, 46, 88
Cailleville, Godebert (also known as
    Caneville) 38
Calais 13, 21, 39, 43, **89**, 91
Camoys, Roger de 48, 75, 77, 80, 82
campaign
    commanders 17–21
    impact on England 88–90

impact on France 84–88
    origin of 5–7
    see also Gascony campaign; Normandy
        campaign
Carentan **26**, 27, **27**, 28–29
Carrachat, Yvonnet 78
carvings **16**, **41**, **43**, **45**, **60**, **85**
Castelnau 77
Castillon, battle of (1453) **50**, **54**, **55**, **59**, **60**
    casualties 71–72
    phase one 51, **52–53**, 54–55, **56–57** (58),
        59–62
    phase two 63–71, **64–65** (66), **68–69**
    surrender and aftermath 72–74
Cathedral of Saint-André (Bordeaux) **47**
Catherine de Valois 5
Chabannes, Jacques de 19, 49, 51, 61, 62,
    72, 73–74, 77
Chalais **50**, 51
Chapel of Saint-Louis (Formigny) **30**
Charles I, Duke of Bourbon 18
Charles VI, King of France 5
Charles VII, King of France
    and Arthur de Richemont 18
    and Charles I, Duke of Bourbon 18
    and the Count of Foix 42
    'French France' 5, 6, 7
    Gascony campaign 48–50, 51, 70, 71,
        73–75, 77, 79, 82–83
    and Jacques Coeur 42
    and Jean Bureau 19
    and John Talbot 46, 62, 72
    as military commander 17, **17**
    military reforms 10–11, **12**
    national reconciliation 84
    and Norman aristocracy 14
    Normandy campaign 22–23, 26, 38–39
    and Pierre II, Duke of Brittany 42
    rise of nationalism 16
    and Yvonnet Carrachat 78
Chartier, Jean 31, 35, 61, 63, **63**, 70–71,
    72, 77
Château du Roi (Saint-Émilion) **59**
Château-Gaillard 23
Cherbourg 26, 27, 28, 39, 45
chevauchée raids 15
Christie, M. B. 19
chronology 8–9
Church of St John the Baptist (Hatch
    Beauchamp) **16**
Clermont, Jean de 17–18, **17**
    Gascony campaign 49, 50, 59, 75, 77,
        79–80
    Normandy campaign 27, 28–31, **31**,
        32–33 (34), 35, 38, 92
Clifton, Gervase 43, 45, 76
Clifton, Thomas 75
Coëtivy, Admiral Prigent de 29, 31, 35,
    39, 45
Coëtivy, Seneschal Alain de 45–46
Coeur, Jacques 42, **45**
Colville, Cuthbert 25
commanders 17–21
Concarneau 46
Courtenay, John 76
Couvran, Geoffroy de 25, 28
Couvran, Guillaume de 28
crossbowman (Franciscan breviary) **61**

Culant, Lord of 49
Cunningham, Robert 31
Curry, Anne 89

des Peaux, René 63
Dieppe 7
Ditcham, B. 86
Domfront 39
Druic, Thomas (also known as Driuc, Drew
    or Dring) 35
Duke of Alençon 23, 84
Duke of Burgundy 7, 22, **41**, 86, 91
Duke of Lorraine 10
Duke of Suffolk 22, 23, 25, **41**, 88
Duke of York 19, 42–43, 82, 88
Dunois, Jean de 23, 38–39, 48
Durfort, Gailhard de, Lord of Duras 75, 77,
    79–80, 82

écorcheurs 10
Edict of Compiègne (1429) 88
Edmund Beaufort, Duke of Somerset 19, 21,
    22–23, 25, 26–27, 28, 39, 43, 82
Edward III, King of England 6, 21, 91
Edward IV, King of England 90, 91
English forces 11–15, **14**, **15**, 19–21
English France **4** (5), 6
English Parliament 7, 12, 21, 25, 47
English Reformation 88, 91
Engranville 38, 92
Escoucy, Matthew d' 92
Evringham, Thomas, Sir 61–62, 63, 67, 72

Falaise 26, 39, **39**, 72, 87
Fastolf, John, Sir 41, 90
Fiennes, James, Lord Say 41
Floquet 31
Foix, Count of see Gaston IV, Count
    of Foix
Formigny, battle of (1450) 29–35, **29**, **30**,
    31, **32–33** (34), **35**, **36–37**, **38**, **39**
fortifications **13**, **15**, **30**, **59**, **63**, **75**, **78**, 82
Fougères 22, 23
François I, Duke of Brittany 22–23,
    27–28, 38
francs-archers **12**
Frederick of Austria (Hapsburg) 10
French civil war (1410–14) 18
French forces 10–11, **11**, **12**, **14**, 15, 17–19,
    85–86
'French France' 5, 6, 7
Fresnay-sur-Sarthe 28
Fronsac 42, 46, 47, 48, 75

Gaillardet 77, 79
gargoyles **48**, **86**
Gascony campaign
    French conquest, phase one 42–51,
        44 (45)
    French conquest, phase two 74–83,
        81 (80)
    impact of French conquest 88
    pro-English sentiments 6, 14, 16, 42, 45,
        46, 67
    see also Castillon, battle of (1453)
Gaston IV, Count of Foix 25, 42, 48, 49, 50,
    59, 75, 77
Gensac 51

Giffart, Olivier 71
Gilles de Bretagne 28
Giribault, Louis 31, 51, 70
Gough, Matthew 21, 26, 29, 30–31, 35
Gower, Thomas 39
Grafton, Richard 26
Grand-Vey estuary, crossing of 27, 28–29
Great Chevauchée (1373) 18
Gruel, Guillaume 35
Guichen 25

Hall, Edward 21
Harfleur, siege of 26
Henry V, King of England 5
Henry VI, King of England
    accession to the throne 5
    Gascony 14, 47
    and John Talbot 20
    Maine 7, 22
    marriage 6
    mental health 82, 88
    reputation 88–89
    and the Yorkists 43
Henry VII, King of England 88
Henry VIII, King of England 88
Herbert, William 38
Honfleur 26
Hull, Edward 43, 45, 46–47, 72, 77
Hunaudaye, Lord of 59, 70
Hundred Years War (1337–1453) 5, 15, 19,
    83, 84, 85, 89, 90–91
Hungerford, Robert, Lord Moleyns 71, 72,
    87, 90

Jalonges, Marshal de 49, 77
Jean II de Brosse 29
Jean V de Bueil 18–19, 49, 51, 62–63, 72,
    73–74, 82
Jeanne d'Arc 5, 17, 18
John of Gaunt 18, 19
Jonsac, siege of 42, 43
Jouvenal des Ursins (family) 73
Jouvencel, Le (Jean de Bueil) 18, 19

Kendall, Lord 62, 70
Kingdom of Bourges 5, 18
Kirkeby, Thomas 35
Kyriell, Thomas, Sir 19, 20, 21, 23, 26–27,
    28–31, 35, 90

La Hire 21
La Rochelle 76, 82
La Trémoille, Bastard of 29
Lancastrians 43, 90
Lautrec, Viscount of 49
le Bouvier, Gilles 35, 62–63, 71, 72
Legend of Troy (mid-15th-century copy) 11,
    14, 75
Lesparre, Lord of 72, 75, 82, 88
Leuven Hôtel de Ville 41
Libourne, siege of 60, 71, 74, 74, 75, 76
L'Isle, Gaston de 77
Lisle, John, Viscount see Talbot, John,
    1st Viscount Lisle
Lohéac, Marshal de 29, 49
Longworth, Elis 38
Lorraine 10
Lot, Ferdinand 29, 60, 67
Louvain, Pierre de 49
Lusignan 48, 50, 51
Luxembourg, Jacques de 29, 38, 39

mail shirt 39
Maine 7, 22, 49, 89
Malestroit, Philippe de 29
Mantes 23
Margaret of Anjou (Queen Margaret) 6, 20,
    21, 23, 43, 82
Mauny, Sire de 31
Messignac, Jean de 46
Metz 10
Moleyns, Adam 25
Moleyns, Lord see Hungerford, Robert, Lord
    Moleyns
Monstrelet, Enguerrant de 67, 70, 72, 73
Montauban, Lord of 59, 70
Montferrant, Bertrand, Lord of 75
Montferrant, Pierre de see Lesparre, Lord of
Montguyon 42

nationalism, rise of 15–16
Norberry, Henry 26, 35
Normandy campaign
    English invasion 26–28
    French reconquest, phase one 22–26,
        24 (25)
    French reconquest, phase two 35, 38–41,
        40 (41)
    impact of French reconquest 86–87,
        89–90
    resistance to English rule 14, 16, 22
    see also Formigny, battle of (1450)

Orléans, siege of (1428-1429) 10
Orval, Lord of 49

Palais de Justice (Paris) 6
Paris 5, 6, 7, 23
Patay, battle of (1429) 18, 21
Perunin, Michael 71
Philippe Auguste, King of France 6
Piccolomini, Aeneas (later Pope Pius II) 60
Pierre II, Duke of Brittany 42, 59
Pollard, A.J. 67
Pont-Audemer 23, 87
Pontièvre, Count of 49, 71
Pontoise 7
Portsmouth 7, 23–25
Powis, Lord 23
Praguerie revolt (1439–40) 18
Priory of Saint-Florent (Castillon) 51, 55,
    56–57 (58), 60–61, 92

Quarter Jacks (Wells Cathedral) 14

Rauzan ford 50, 51, 71
Rauzan, Lord of 72, 75
René, King of Sicily 38
Richard I, King of England 6
Richemont, Arthur (III) de 7, 17, 18, 18
    Normandy campaign 22, 27–28, 29, 31,
        31, 32–33 (34), 35, 38
Roche-Guyon 23, 86
Rouault, Abel 26–27
Rouault, Joachim 17, 86, 90
    Gascony campaign 46–49, 51, 61, 63, 78
    Normandy campaign 25, 26, 28
Rouen 23
Ry 21

St Albans, first battle of (1455) 19, 91
St Albans, second battle of (1461) 21
Saint-Belin, Geoffrey de 49

Saint-Émilion 59, 60, 71, 74, 76
Saint-Lô 28, 38
St Mary Magdalene Church, Battlefield
    48, 86
St Maurice (warrior) 60
Saint-Simon, Gilles de 29
Savoy 43
Say, Lord 82
    see also Fiennes, James, Lord Say
Scotland 22
seal of John Holland 15
ship carvings 45
Shrewsbury, battle of (1403) 48
Shrewsbury Book 20
Solon, P.D. 78
Sorbier, Louis 63
Sorel, Agnes 17, 18, 26, 42
Story of Roland 49
Surienne, François de 22
Swynford, Katherine 19

tabards 25, 85
Talbot, John, 1st Earl of Shrewsbury
    biography 21, 73, 77
    death of 67, 70, 71, 72
    Gascony campaign 43, 45–47, 48, 49,
        50–51
    Gascony campaign (Castillon) 59–63, 67,
        70–71, 80, 92
    Normandy campaign 23, 39
    receiving sword from Henry VI 20
    and Thomas Kyriell 19
Talbot, John, 1st Viscount Lisle 47–48, 49,
    70, 71, 72, 76
tapestries 61, 79, 85
Thevet, André 73
Treaty of Troyes (1420) 5, 6
Trévières 29, 31, 92
Truce of Picquigny (1475) 91
Truce of Tours (1444) 7, 10

Valognes 23, 26–27, 28, 39
Valpergue, Boniface de 46, 49, 74
Valpergue, Theaulde 79
Vere, Robert 26, 35
Verneuil 22–23
Vignier 71–72
Villon, François 18
Vire 25, 26, 38
Viriville, Vallet de 71
Viscount Lisle see Talbot, John, 1st Viscount
    Lisle

Wars of the Roses 19, 88–89, 90, 91
weapons
    cannons 61, 67
    Castillon swords 73, 88
    crossbow 61
    English armies 15, 28
    French armies 10, 11, 55, 62
    hand-held guns 51, 67, 79
    veuglair 13
Wells Cathedral Quarter Jacks 14
Westenhanger castle (Kent) 19, 20
Witz, Konrad 16
Woodville, Richard, Lord Rivers 42
Worcester, William 90

Xaintrailles, Jean Poton de 21, 49, 77

Yorkists 19, 21, 42–43, 90